MW01675720

The Talking Stick

Volume Sixteen

Finding the Words

A publication of the
Jackpine Writers' Bloc
www.jackpinewriters.com
www.thetalkingstick.com

We thank iStockphoto.com for connecting us with the talented photographers included in this book.

Send correspondence to Jackpine Writers' Bloc,
13320 149th Ave, Menahga, Minnesota 56464.
sharrick1@wcta.net
www.jackpinewriters.com www.thetalkingstick.com

Printed in the U.S.A
by Morris Publishing, Kearney NE

ISBN: 978-1-928690-08-5

Table of Contents
Poetry, Creative Nonfiction and Fiction

Poetry, Creative Nonfiction and Fiction

Poetry, Creative Nonfiction and Fiction

Poetry, Creative Nonfiction and Fiction

Co-Editor's Note

Tarah L. Wolff

Editor's Choice: When Soda Always Came In Glass Bottles by Margarette Hasse, page 161

This is the first year we included in the Talking Stick an "Editor's Choice" award. It does not involve a money prize or a prize of any kind for the author. It is really just for the editors (little ol' me and Sharon Harris) so we can point out one piece we did not feel got the recognition it deserved.

I chose *When Soda Always Came in Glass Bottles* by Margaret Hasse. I thought with this choice I had to be careful in a sense. I thought, perhaps people would read my Editor's Choice and think, "Maybe I can learn from this," or, "Maybe this is what they're looking for in the Talking Stick." And the truth is a resounding, *YES*. This choice of mine is a good example of what I look for in writing (not just poetry). Margaret, in this poem, uses words clearly, precisely and uniquely. Her comparisons are creative and the ending of her poem will stop your heart. If you notice, there is, in no place, a repeat of what she is trying to say; instead, she trusted the images she gave the reader and let the dominoes fall.

Our winners this year are good examples of how not much needs to be said for a lot to fall on the table. I was ecstatic when *Because* won first place Fiction because it was one of the shortest pieces submitted for fiction this year. It is an excellent example of intelligent cutting, something I daresay we all could probably use more of . . .

I was left this year with the image of our writers in big domed, dark rooms alone, setting out dominoes long into the night. And when it was time for the single finger flick for the art to come alive, they turned to leave. I can see them smiling, no anxiety, blindly abandoning their "darlings." The writers understand that being there to explain it won't make it any more lovely, that being there to "help" the dominoes fall would accomplish nothing. Their dominoes go out into the world alone. Until they are picked up by a reader one night and, with a single finger flick, they become perfect.

Co-Editor's Note

Sharon Harris

Editor's Choice: Mated
by Harriet Duerre, page 134

This is the fifth book that I have co-edited with my niece Tarah Wolff. As always, this is exhausting but rewarding. Somehow, between workshops and other writing events, we find minutes here and there to complete the proof-reading, ponder the layout, etc. For Talking Stick 16, we received 249 submissions from 118 different writers. We selected 87 poems, 15 creative nonfiction pieces, and 19 fiction stories by 88 different writers for the book. We actually had a few less entries than last year, but the quality seemed to be even better. This book will be 228 pages, slightly larger than last year.

This year, Tarah and I decided that we would each choose our favorite submission. My Editor's Choice is *Mated* by Harriet Duerre.

I always fall for poems about lasting love, growing old together, mating for life. I grew up with the idea that you meet one man and fall in love and live happily ever after. I was never going to get divorced, to have to find another. I still like to believe in that. I had so hoped that my marriage would be my last relationship, with us "changing from young to old, trading leads through storm and brilliance, taking great gulps of the sky, never envisioning the final touchdown." I had hoped that I would end this life with a beloved spouse of many years holding my hand as I slipped away.

Thinking of losing a long loved spouse or parent or friend reminds me of an old proverb I heard recently: *When someone dies, a library burns.*

When you lose someone you love, their store of knowledge, experience and wisdom passes out of the world. All their stories, all their history, the thoughts, the memories, the joys, the regrets, all gone —unless someone recorded them. If a person writes their own personal memoir, that is priceless, even if it never leaves the family. Some are so memorable they can become best sellers. We all like to hear how other people lived and loved. And if we can see parts of ourselves in those stories, so much the better.

We all have unique experiences, we all have unique reasons for being here, for leaving our fingerprints on the lives of our loved ones. If you didn't tell someone the fabulous thing that happened to you when you were 20 or when you were 35, then it is gone. It is almost as if it had never happened. You want the record of your experiences to last longer than you will, so that what you did here mattered.

Don't take your stories with you. After you are gone, who will tell your stories?

The Judges

Poetry Judge: CarolAnn Russell

CarolAnn Russell has published three full-length books of poetry: *The Red Envelope* (University Presses of Florida, 1985), *Feast* (Loonfeather Press, Minnesota 1993) and *Silver Dollar* (West End Press, Albuquerque, New Mexico, 1995). In addition, she has published three limited editions of poetry. Russell has also won many awards and grants for her poetry. She lives in northern Minnesota with her husband, Michael Schlemper, their two sons Josef and Zoey, and two cats. Russell is Professor of Creative Writing and Women's Studies in the Department of English at Bemidji State University.

Creative Nonfiction Judge: Bill Holm

Bill Holm was born in 1943 on a farm north of Minneota, Minnesota. He continues to live in Minneota half the year while he teaches at Southwest State University in Marshall. He spends his summers at his little house on a northern Iceland fjord where he writes, practices the piano, and waits for the first dark after three months of daylight. He is the author of several books, both poetry and essays, including *Playing the Black Piano*, *Coming Home Crazy* and *Eccentric Islands*.

Fiction Judge: William Kent Krueger

William Kent Krueger was raised in Oregon. He briefly attended Stanford University. Later, he logged timber, worked construction, tried free-lance journalism, and ended up researching child development at the University of MN. He now makes his living as a full-time author. With his wife of 34 years and their two children, he lives in St. Paul, MN. Krueger writes a mystery series set in the north woods of Minnesota. His protagonist is Cork O'Connor, the former sheriff of Tamarack County and a man of mixed heritage—part Irish and part Ojibwe. Krueger has won numerous awards for his novels, and his work has been optioned by Hollywood. He does all his creative writing in booth #4 in the St. Clair Broiler in St. Paul.

List of Winners

Poetry

Judged by CarolAnn Russell

First Place $500: shrapnel by Kathleen Lindstrom

For twenty-five years, Kathleen Lindstrom was an award-winning writer in Communications and PR departments. She started to "follow her bliss" three years ago by delving into the world of creative fiction. Since that time, one of her stories won second place in the *2006 Arthur Edelstein Prize for Short Fiction*. Other stories have been published in *Megaera Magazine*, *The Talking Stick*, *Aesthetica Magazine*, *The Sidewalk's End*, *Words Words Words*, *Lily Literary Magazine*, *Ancient Paths*, *Flashquake* and *St. Anthony's Messenger*.

Second Place: Laundry Day by Marianne McNamara

Honorable Mention:

Myownhorn by Ronald Gower
The Old Fence Row by Luke Anderson
Dirty Hands by Larry Schug
Last House on the Road by Thomas C. Stetzler
Onion Tears by Marlene Mattila Stoehr

List of Winners

Creative Nonfiction

Judged by Bill Holm

First Place $500: How Mother Came to Float Down the St. Croix by Peter Schwarz

Peter Schwarz was born in Germany. He later lived in Switz-erland and Palestine/Israel. He came to the U.S. in 1957, attended the University of Minnesota, and married a Minneapolis girl. He has been retired since 1992. His work history includes: Child actor, musician, photographer, advertising/writer/journalist.

Second Place: Gone to the Dogs by Connie Claire Szarka

Honorable Mention:

Montana Roads by Lorna Rafness
Life's Cycle by Julia Klebs
Sole Searching by Mary Lynn Regnier

List of Winners

Fiction

Judged by William Kent Krueger

First Place $500: Because by Barbara Jacksha

Barbara Jacksha is a freelance writer and an editor and co-founder of the literary journal *Cezanne's Carrot*. Her work has appeared in the recent W. W. Norton anthology *Flash Fiction Forward* and has been nominated twice for the Pushcart Prize. Barbara's work has also been published in a variety of print and online journals, including *Beloit Fiction Journal*, *The Summerset Review*, *Peregrine*, *VOX*, *Per Contra*, *Mindprints*, *Poetry Midwest*, *The Talking Stick*, *Carve Magazine*, *Tattoo Highway*, *Smokelong Quarterly*, *The Rockford Review*, *The Steel City Review*, and *Quercus Review*. Barbara is a native Minnesotan, married to a native Iron Ranger, now living near Santa Fe, New Mexico.

Second Place: Motel Six by Jeanne Weber

Honorable Mention:

The Day the Nuns Wore Dresses
Bergdorf, North Dakota 1948
by Niomi Rohn Phillips
Dirty Indians by Anne M. Dunn
Faded Images by Kathleen Free
History Stains by Susan Wolter Nettell

Finding the Words

Poetry – First Place
by Kathleen Lindstrom

shrapnel

we walk a prickly path
in this house
lush with lavender rugs
and plastic Picassos
and hugs at the proper time
and meals steamed with
carrots and a silence
that slices through our hearts
like hot knives on soft butter

but it won't take much
we are up for the thrill
we can smell the minefield
in his mournful eyes

we are his children, after all

the treacherous path
lures us on
like the lurid smile of a broken prize
found deep in the heart of a happy meal
    one greasy look
    one prodding poke
    one biting word
and we trip the wire of his worn-down soul

then watch him detonate like a dying star
like an oceanic, atomic blast
surging outward, at us, for us
a titanic burst of fire and flame
piercing us
with particles of his grief
his self-loathing
his dried-up longings, his lacerated heart

then he bolts from the room like an aftershock
leaving behind the residue of rage
spiked memories puncturing our hearts
　　　　shards of hurt
　　　　splinters of pain
　　　　slivers of grief
wounds that don't heal
scars that still shimmer with shame

he is our father, after all

Creative Nonfiction – First Place
by Peter Schwarz

How Mother Came to Float Down the St. Croix

You ought to know upfront that Mother is dead. Has been for almost twenty years now. She passed away in 1988 and was cremated. It's what she wanted. We had a nice memorial service at the funeral home, with organ music. After that, we couldn't decide what to do with her ashes. Ordinarily the place of honor for an urn would be the mantle. But we had no fireplace, not even a fake one, and so, no mantle. We briefly considered placing the urn on top of the refrigerator, or on the bookshelf, next to where we stashed the bills, or the cupboard with the canned goods, but none of these seemed appropriately dignified. There was room on my dresser, but we just couldn't have Mother in the bedroom with us at all times. Nor could we bury the urn because, you see, Mother was from Berlin, Germany, and one of her wishes was to be returned to her birthplace and have her ashes spread on Lake Havel. Finally, we left the urn with the funeral home, where it stayed for the next twelve years.

When I was invited to Berlin in 2000, it seemed the perfect opportunity to also take Mother. Because I'm aware of the Teutonic penchant for strict regulations, I thought it wise to first call the German embassy in Chicago, and find out exactly what they'd require. The receptionist connected me with an official in charge of travel visas. First, he advised that German or U.S. citizens require no visa, but on learning that Mother was dead, he said it exceeded his area of expertise, and had me transferred to a specialist.

If memory serves, it was a Frau Hauser, whose authority and competence extended to expired people, funerals, and doubtlessly, other societal issues. She listened to my query attentively and with a sympathetic ear, asked some pertinent questions which I apparently answered to her satisfaction. Frau Hauser advised that I'll need Mother's birth certificate, her German passport, a certified copy of the death certificate and a letter from the funeral home, verifying that Mother had never left the premises since she was cremated.

I worried that explaining this to the funeral home might be a problem, but they were familiar with it. They issue such letters routinely, whenever the remains of one of their clients are to be transported. It just goes to show how little I knew about the junkets of the departed.

When traveling, I pack lightly, one suitcase, preferably small. The urn was in a separate package, replete with carrying handle. On arrival at Tegel airport in Berlin, the customs officer never even looked at my suitcase. All he wanted to know was what was in that package.

"This is my Mother," I said. He looked perplexed, so I helpfully added, "Her ashes. She's dead."

"Aha, it is an urn!" he crowed, and I nodded.

"What do you intend to do with it?" he asked.

"She was born here in Berlin," I explained, "and she wanted to be returned to her place of birth. I'm going to spread her ashes on Lake Havel."

"Impossible," he exclaimed with a horrified expression. "There are regulations and this is against the law."

"You can't spread ashes on the lake? Is it a new law? Frau Hauser, the funeral expert at the German Embassy, never mentioned it. And I have all the required papers."

"No, the law is not new. And the papers only identify the deceased, but do not give you permission to spread the ashes on a lake."

"Well then, maybe I could dispose of her ashes in the Schöneberg park, where we used to live. She loved this park."

"No, no. You cannot do anything like that. Your Mother's ashes have to be buried in a cemetery."

"OK then, if that is the only option, that's what I'll do." No point in arguing with a bureaucrat. A *uniformed* bureaucrat at that. Once out of customs, I'd take her to the lake, and if need be, spread the ashes at night. I reached for the packaged urn but he quickly stopped me.

"No, you cannot take this with you. You'll have to contact a funeral service. Only they can take possession of the urn and inter it. Make some phone calls. There are many good funeral homes in the city; they'll take care of you."

"What do I do with Mother in the meantime?"

"We'll keep the urn here and give you a receipt. Keep in mind that after 30 days, we dispose of all unclaimed materials."

I didn't think to ask what "dispose of" meant. Or maybe I didn't really want to know. It was obvious by now that the authorities wouldn't go for a do-it-yourself burial. So I called a funeral home and explained my dilemma. The funeral guy spoke in measured cadence, with a well modulated voice, befitting the somber occasion.

"Where is your Mother now?" he asked.

"She's in custody," I said, "with customs."

"First we'll have to get the urn released. But we know how to do that; there will be no problem. Then what are your plans?"

"Could we spread the ashes on Lake Havel?" It was stupid, I know, but I had to try.

"Impossible," he said. "You cannot spread ashes anywhere. It's against the law."

"I guess we'll have to bury the urn," I said.

"Yes, I think so. Do you have a cemetery preference?"

"No, I don't really know the city very well. Do you have a suggestion?"

"It depends. Would you be interested in a family plot?"

"Family plot? It's only my Mother. There is no one else."

"What about yourself, and your family? Have you thought about that?"

"We live half way around the world. I think we'll stay there."

"What religion was your Mother?"

"Religion? Lutheran. Why do you ask?"

"To select the appropriate clergy for the service."

"She was not religious. I don't think we need a service. We had a memorial."

"It's tradition," he said, "and do you have any idea how many will attend the funeral?"

"Yes, just me."

"What about other relatives, friends, acquaintances, coworkers?"

"All the family is long gone, and she left here in 1933. I don't think there is anyone who knows her."

"We'll plan on a small chapel then. What kind of music would you like?"

"What do you mean *music*?" My patience was running thin, and I had a sense he was trying to sell me on a string quartet. "She's been dead for a dozen years. We had a memorial service, then, *with music*. We don't *need* music for the ashes."

"This is how a *proper* funeral service is done here," he said haughtily. "We have some very nice CDs and you can choose what you want. No extra charge."

Had we been face to face, I think he would have spanked me.

"How much is all this going to cost?" I asked.

"Well, let's see," he proceeded to mumble, letting me hear it: " . . . forms for customs release, transport urn to chapel, chapel rent, pastor fees, music . . .

"What about flowers? You want flowers, perhaps a wreath?"

"OK, a nice flower arrangement."

"Just one, right?" He didn't wait for my answer and kept mumbling, " . . . flowers, announcements, documents . . .

"What about a headstone? You want to order one now or wait till later?"

"Later. I'll order one later." I didn't tell him it wouldn't be in his lifetime.

" . . . Hearse, plot, excavation, tax, gratuity . . . " Finally he quoted a figure. More than twice what I had expected. Way more. "I'll have to think about it," I said, and hung up.

The price was a bit steep, but it wasn't just about the money. Mother wanted her ashes spread on the lake because she had fond memories of the place, its beauty, and happy times there as a child. She said she didn't want to be buried. Not where no one who knew her would ever visit, where no one would tend the grave.

Returning to customs, I told the officer that I'd take Mother back to the States with me. "I'm sorry," he said, "but again, I cannot release the urn to you." He actually sounded contrite.

"Well then, tell me what I *can* do. How do I get Mother back home?"

He thought for a while. "The best way, probably the only way, is to ship the urn. There is a post office right here at the airport. You could ship the urn from there."

It had never occurred to me to just mail Mother. But it seemed a simple, workable solution. "Fine," I said. "How do I get the urn to the post office?"

He looked at the clock. "The post office is still open. I'll assign someone to carry the urn. You'll have to go with him and pay the postage and such."

"Excellent. I'd appreciate it if we can take care of this now."

And so Mother was shipped home. I didn't know what to expect. What would U.S. customs have to say? Would they let her back in the country? I had visions of Mother shuttling back and forth between customs across the Atlantic, as in the odyssey of the *Flying Dutchman*, condemned to everlasting voyage, never to alight.

Some three weeks after I'd returned home, the mailman knocked and set the dog to barking. By the time I went to the door, he left some letters, a magazine, and Mother. There she sat, all packaged up. No one had bothered to check the contents. No one questioned her right to be here, or challenged what I might do with her ashes. Just one of the little iconic attributes of a free society—though it may not play today, what with Homeland Security, the Patriot Act, and all.

A few months later, my son Perry came to visit from the west coast. On a warm autumn afternoon, we sat on a rocky ledge on the Minnesota side of the river. Perry reminisced about his Grandma, and I about Mother. Then we slowly spilled her ashes into the river. There wasn't much. One by one, we tossed a dozen roses on the water, and quietly watched Mother float down the St. Croix.

Fiction – First Place

by Barbara Jacksha

Because

When he left, it was not because she hated the way he traced the star-field freckles on her knee, or because she left slips of hair curled like dead eels around the shower drain. It was not because she shuddered when she cried. Or because her hips, once again boney and protruding, no longer bumped gently against his.

When he left, he took the flat-screen TV, the surround-sound system, the dumbbell set, the stretched-hide drum, and guitar. She claimed he chose the remaining precious things, but it was not a matter of value. He wanted distraction, noise; he understood density, weight.

He left her the quiet room, the dusty doorknob neither of them would touch.

When he left, it was not because there'd been a child—because they saw the sun chased by pink clouds, felt bellybutton kisses brush their cheeks, heard breathy puffs that reminded them of elves and the sound of nickering does on the breeze.

It wasn't even the stiff-snake lights at the emergency room. The doctor's voice. Words that grew horns. He remembered the feeling. Both of them crumpling like paper—folded, creased, thrown on choppy water before they even thought to breathe. He'd watched her drift away, a paper sailboat slipping off the edge of the sea with newsprint for a rudder and not a single flapping sheet to raise against the wind. But when he left, it was not because of this.

The month before he left, he found an empty bed at two a.m. He searched for hours, finally finding her pacing the tennis court on the hilltop, the only place wide enough to hold her scream.

The day he left, he picked at his breakfast, poured swollen cereal down the wrong side of the sink. When he turned from her, it was not because she sighed as she scooped out milky, sodden flakes. It was not because she'd finally stopped howling. It was not because she'd relearned how to blink in the sunlight or remembered how to pronounce her own name.

It was not because he thought she'd conceive again.

If he dared, he'd lead her back to the tennis court, to the trees where he watched from the wild side of the fence. He'd tell her that when she screamed, he heard only the leafy shush of shadows and the torn net snapping like a bat with broken wings.

If he could, he'd say he saw her howl—an anaconda snaking upward, tongue flicking, tasting black. He'd describe how it arced through the stars before angling earthward. How it shot down and burrowed into his chest. How inside, her howl was met by one of his.

When he left, he said it was because of the shuddering cries, the dead-eel hair, the dusty doorway. But if he could, he would have cracked open his ribs, showed her the twin anacondas, twin howls, weighing down his chest.

When he left, it was because he'd seen an ease returning to her movements, heard a breathy glide in her sighs. She was the sailboat tacking a course toward calmer waters—while he was the drag of twin-fanged anchors, drifting deeper and far from rest.

Poetry – Second Place

by Marianne McNamara

Laundry Day

Ma washed on Mondays
heavy cotton sheets, towels
and fancy embroidered pillow cases
strung out to dry on the old rope
between the oak and sugar maple in our backyard,

a brown-eyed baby on one hip
bursting laundry basket on the other,
tiny socks poking through frayed willow holes,
wooden clothespins in her apron pocket
and one or two in her mouth like straight pins
porcupining from a pincushion.

The maple was a good climbing tree
and while Ma tacked up dripping bedclothes
I'd scramble to my lookout post,
the skipper navigating swirling grass green seas.
The breeze billowed the sun-bleached sheets,
flapped and filled them like the sails on a schooner,

whipped the make-believe waves into whitecaps of meringue,
collided them over and over against the sandy shore.
Best of all was the sweet smell of the bedclothes
when Ma unpegged the sails
and tucked them back on our beds.

Creative Nonfiction – Second Place
by Connie Claire Szarka

Gone to the Dogs

> "If a dog will not come to you after he has looked you in the face, you should go home and examine your conscience."
>
> —Woodrow Wilson

"I'm not going to rescue you if you go down. He's most likely dead anyway."

It was first light on a cold Monday morning. The instant I cracked open the lakeside door, an icy wind chased dust balls and loose papers across the hardwood floor and tipped over a faded snapshot of my husband and me.

"Who needs you," I growled back at him.

"You're a fool," he countered. "Why don't you think for a change? Stay put. Besides, you'll be late for work."

Lately, wherever I went, my husband cast a mean word after me. I curled my lip, then made my way down the steps, across the yard, and down our snow-packed hill.

The temperature hovered at ten below plus wind chill—unusually cold for March. (Chilly inside the house, too, before the furnace could kick in.) I grabbed a long stick from the woodpile on shore and jabbed it ahead of me as I stepped onto the frozen bay. If the stick went through, I'd have to find an alternate path, a section of ice still thick enough to bear my weight. Once I'd made it across the slab closest to land, I'd be safer. But because we'd had enough mild days and rain to begin the rotting process, you never knew for sure which parts of the lake were weak and honeycombed.

Paying attention to color and consistency and the sound of my stick against that great block were all I had to go on as I inched toward my destination: a dark, still lump in the middle of the bay. I wondered if the animal had survived the piercingly cold and windy hours of the night.

I'd first noticed the small black and white dog around noon on Sunday, running up and down the long stretch of West Arm Bay. I trained my binoculars on him. It pleased me to witness such exuberant play in a Sheltie herding dead leaves fluttering across the surface. He was just getting his exercise after being cooped up all morning. I smiled and went about my business.

By mid-aftemoon, however, the dog was still running. Only now he seemed confused, as if searching for something or someone. I hiked down to the shore and called out to him, tried to coax him in. But he veered off and kept sweeping along the ice until I thought he'd run his heart out.

Scanning the shoreline, I focused on a cluster of people at the other end of the lake. Some stood rigid while others pushed a yellow and blue inflatable ahead of them. The dog skittered in the opposite direction each time they got near.

I jumped into my car, pumped the gas pedal until the sluggish engine ground to a start, and drove around the bay. After many turns on narrow streets, I located the neighborhood where the rescue team had gathered.

"We're supposed to be dog-sitting," cried a woman whose husband was equally concerned. "His name is Nick. We've been trying to catch him all day."

I joined in, calling the dog's name over and over while two men from the fire department scooted around behind their raft. The ice was more unstable on this side, near the cove.

"It's impossible," said one. "We don't dare chase after him on foot much less on a machine."

"Even if we did," said the other, "he'd take off again. He's definitely disoriented, probably looking for home, something familiar."

Home for Nick was on a bay in northern Minnesota, not here on Lake Minnetonka, where oversized houses took up most of the land. And his humans were in Hawaii.

Although the outcome remained uncertain, there was something beautiful about Nick skimming over the ice as if sailing on a steady breeze, ignoring peoples' desperate commands to stop, sit, stay. Even though he didn't know where he was going, he was free.

I returned home, saddened by our failure to catch the dog, but heartened by the actions of caring men.

At dusk, Nick was still running, except at a much slower pace and stopping often to gaze about. Then, as night fell, he lay down on the ice, in the open, with his back to a bitter wind.

I kept vigil from my bedroom window, squinting into the darkness until I could no longer see what looked like a small boulder in the middle of that broad, white expanse. I went to bed imagining the slow death of this exhausted animal.

First thing next morning, I set out on my hike, cautious as I crossed the bay with the words, *I'm not going to rescue you if you go down* running through my mind like a stuck record. I was determined not to go down. But if I did, I felt certain that I'd be able to break ice and kick my legs until I could raise myself up and out . . . that is, unless hypothermia got to me first.

From a distance, I saw no movement in the dark mound of a dog. No sign of life. It didn't surprise me. How could any being, even one with a triple coat, survive such a night without shelter?

I could hardly bear to admit that my husband had probably been right. Yet, even though Nick might be dead, I couldn't leave him lying out there on the ice. I realized then how unprepared I was, having left the house wearing only a jacket. No hat, no gloves, and nothing to wrap around the little dog. Perhaps my husband was watching out for us after all, waiting with a warm blanket, ready to mourn with me or to celebrate. But I couldn't count on it.

As I approached the dog, his head moved slightly. Then he focused his eyes on me and made an effort to stand. But he wasn't able to move. I tried to pick him up, but couldn't. The warmth of Nick's body had melted the ice enough to refreeze onto long strands of belly hair as well as the shorter fur beneath his forelegs. Nick was stuck.

With nothing to cut him free, I set to work peeling him away one layer at a time, several hairs at a time.

"Good boy, Nicky. You'll be fine," I crooned while tugging at his fur, some by the roots, which must have hurt him terribly. Yet, he never snapped at me or even whimpered. He just went limp and rested his muzzle on the ice. "We'll make it, Nick. We're gonna make it."

Then I remembered the car keys in my jacket pocket and used them to saw forth and back, first at the hair along his legs, then at the belly fur. I sawed and pulled and peeled and when we were finished, we'd left several black and white clumps behind, still clinging to the molded ice. I snatched Nick up before he could bolt again (although he seemed to have little inclination), bundled him inside my coat, and started for home along my proven path.

Above the sounds of my own labored breathing, I heard cries from the shore behind me, "Have you seen a little dog?"

"Yes, I have him!" I shouted back. "Follow me!"

Although I knew these were the dog-sitters, I was reluctant to stop until I had Nick safely inside.

I'd given the dog a rubdown and filled a bowl with water by the time the couple had rushed across the last stretch of ice, up the hillside, and into the house. Exhausted and elated that Nick was alive, the woman cried and laughed at the same time. So did her husband. I stood next to them just inside the lakeside door while they took tums cuddling the dog.

My husband, whom Nick had warily approached, then shied away from, was on his way out the back door. He turned briefly. "You were lucky," he said with a half smile. "A lucky fool."

"We want to pay you," said the woman.

"Yes, yes," said the man, reaching for his wallet.

I refused and for a bit of time the three of us watched Nick lap up water and prance around the living room.

Two days later, the receptionist at work summoned me.

"There's a surprise here for you," she said in a happy voice. "Just delivered."

As I approached the main office, I saw the red splash of a dozen roses above the counter. The receptionist, standing beside her desk, was wearing a *you-devil-you* grin.

"I peeked at the card," she said. "'*To Connie, With Love, From Nick*' . . . who's Nick?"

I smiled at her and said, "The beginning of something fine."

Fiction – Second Place
by Jeanne Weber

Motel Six

The unraveling begins. Last night my mother died. Now I long to play dead; my breathing shallow, eyes closed, wanting to cling to Sarah like a baby opossum to its mother—which would be a role reversal, unseemly somehow since I'm Sarah's mother and she's my adult daughter. But since my mother's death, I'm no longer composed of whole cloth. Pieces of me went with her. The nest, now barren, is empty, yet questions remain: where did you go, can you still see me, hear me? I love you, Mom. How many times those words went missing. A bell rings, the game's called—arbitrarily it seems—then a tired voice drones, *time to leave the building, have a safe trip home*. So, Sarah, please help me. Now, through these rags of unraveling, you're the only person to whom I can turn.

The air in the motel corridor is rank, and not surprisingly our room is no better; condensation runs down the only window—which is sealed shut. I turn the air on high as Sarah rounds up two plastic glasses. She breaks a fingernail opening the pour spout on the box of Paul Masson Mountain Red.

"Oh, shit," she says, the accent on the second word. She examines her manicure as she pours two full glasses of wine, giving me one. The television is attached high up on the wall at a crick-in-the-neck angle. Sarah finds the remote. Click. The screen comes to life, a luminous eye staring down at us. She finds one of those stalker movies, flops on the bed and raises her wineglass. "Tits up, Mom," she says with a mischievous grin.

"My goodness. Sarah, for God's sake. Please."

"Lighten up, Mom."

"Just . . . turn that thing off."

"I need it, Mom. I need the distraction. Besides, I'm starving. Why couldn't we stay at a motel with a restaurant?" The edge in her voice ramps to a diesel-whine. She gives me a withering look. Reluctantly, she punches the mute button, while I leave to wander the motel corridors, guided by the din of a distant ice machine. Well, Sarah, match point, but I wonder who's the winner?

Distraction and food sustain the deep hunger of death. I feed the vending machine crisp, green dollar bills and in return receive Cheez Curlz, Salt & Vinegar Chips, Fritos. Serendipitous: Add wine from the box and we have the grace, if not the blessing, of instant communion. I know that between the red wine and the sodium, morning will find me in a state of regret. And there will be cigarettes for dessert. Sarah's a nurse. Luckily, nurses always smoke so I can bum cigarettes from her.

Until now, loss lingered elusively in the past just beyond the scrim, to be measured not by the amount of pain, but by size—huge, so-so, microscopic: a button, an earring, my humor, a few pounds, a beloved pet, my perspective, my mind, my way. I measured loss, dealt with it and got back on track. When death came—to grandparents, aunts, uncles—usually elderly and disconnected from my life by age and distance—I felt a touch of sadness or concern, but nothing more. The death of my mother, however, hangs resolute, filling the present, crowding the room, negating the future. At this moment I am particularly thankful for my prickly Sarah. We are genetically conjoined, linked by the maternal apron string of the umbilical. And Sarah's an oncology nurse. She's seen death.

"Talk to me about death, Sarah. Baby, tell me what happens."

"Oh, Mom," Sarah's voice quavers; obviously she's as devastated as I am. "Why didn't you tell me this would be so hard?"

Sitting on the bed together, we hug. I feel massive waves of sadness surge through Sarah's body.

"Loss is subjective, Sarah—like a game. You're tagged. You're it. The game gets rough."

Together in grief, we hold each other. Her tiny, small-boned body is no longer baby soft but compact, her muscles yoga-hardened. How did this happen? When did I forget this? The feel of my Sarah.

I welcome the distraction of the muted television screen. Commercials flip, flash, vivid, bright. Television, you sly and stealthy weasel, I loathe you, I love you, I hate you. Engrossed, I lip read trying to make sense, to understand, anything to blunt feeling. The absence of sound is the most powerful force in the room. Where is the sound? Where are you?

Sarah's talking. " . . . it's not about games, Mom. I'm not a child. Just listen to me. Please. You never listen to me."

"Listen?" I say, trying to corral my thoughts, to stay in the moment. I want answers. "Okay. But I need to talk about this. About death. What do you think happens?"

"Oh, Mom," Sarah interrupts, snuffles. "I don't know what happens. I miss Grandma, you know. But . . . "

"Sarah, I need to visualize this to make it real. My mother dies—now she's—I don't know. I'm trying to follow her, to see her. How does she get there? She has no wings."

Long ago on a hot summer's day when I was a child, I spent hours sitting in the alley dressed in my nurse's uniform and cap, pulling the delicate wings from lake flies. This operation didn't appear to bother them even though they wriggled mightily in my fingers trying to get away from me; wingless, they wobbled about like stumblebums. This horrified my mother. She lectured me on the spot, right in front of God and the mailman and Mrs. Stock who was hanging her wash on the clothesline. I've forgotten what Mom said to me. The sound of her voice is gone too.

"She has no wings? Really, Mom." Her voice is cheerless. "Grandma, you mean?" Sarah hiccups and her eyes puddle. "Why didn't you tell me, Mom? You never really told me, we didn't talk about . . . " She lights a cigarette—now she has two going in the ashtray. I relieve her of one of them.

"Sarah, now what are you talking about?"

"Marriage, Mom. Marriage can be death, too. Love goes and freedom and passion. Marriage is the pits. It's boring. How did you and Daddy survive?" She looks at me like I've become some kind of mutant.

Survive? I'm speechless. "Sarah, for heaven's sake, you were there. How about the good times? You lived with us for eighteen years."

"Mom, when you were eighteen you slow danced to doo-wop in someone's basement rec room. With the lights off. Big deal. Watching Elvis shake his booty on Ed Sullivan was your version of really hot. College was about getting your MRS degree. Those were your exact words. And none of that mattered. Did it?"

Selective remembering or whatever psychologists call it

—Sarah's honed to an art form. Never talked? Talking with Sarah was akin to chewing roofing nails. Sarah embraced conflict, got off on it, as she would say. My resolution? Silence. Sweet silence. My candy-coated mute button.

Sweet and huggable as a youngster, Sarah, the teenager, existed in another zone: doors slammed, rules hashed, the terrible thrill-ride of leaving childhood behind. In any event, she left us, emotionally, way before her eighteenth year.

Before her wedding, Sarah practiced serial monogamy, enjoying the dating game played with predatory skill, the thrill of the hunt, the courting and lovely sex—then on to the next. With the wedding, our mantra became cautious optimism and heartfelt prayers for our voracious wild-child. Something, maybe the marriage license or the vows or the Tupperware or the forever aspect—something finally got to her, causing her to feel the pinch of matrimony. Now, she mourns the void in her life. I'm no help. My head is spinning.

Ed Sullivan. Lake flies. Past tense. How about priorities? That's not what you want to hear, right Sarah? What have I given up? Cigarettes and bridge, shoulder pads, Transcendental Meditation, wine, annoying relatives. Tennis. Wishing on a star. The feel of you. Mom time. That's a whole laundry list. Our lives aren't parallel. I realize that you're not asking for approval. What are you really saying? You look at me, your tears streaming, and I see a toddler whose dolly's head has come off. Same look. Same tears. And, as always, I am heartsick; seeing your pain cuts me to the bone.

"Sarah, you're right—about our talking. My mother didn't talk to me either. She surprised me with a blush pink peignoir set for my honeymoon. Wow, that just blew me away. Gold metallic slippers, too."

"A peignoir? God, Mom, that's so fifties. You bought me a long flannel nightgown for my honeymoon." This makes us both sputter with laughter.

I resist the urge to say hang in there. Or beware of truths that trip easily off the tongue, Sarah. Truths so prickly they draw blood. One-liners from a stale fortune cookie. Will morning bring clarity?

Come back. I miss you. Call if you can.

Poetry
by Jamie Buehner

Sepia

As if caught on an old
tape of memories

that never got edited,

the streetlights
are about to come on.

The world

is backing further
and further

away.

Banjul, Gambia

Poetry

by Linda Back McKay

River Prayer

The old man was not really in a rowboat
under the Mississippi River bridge.
He was in the process of turning
inside himself, as we all will do one day.

Inside, he was finalizing the finished
and unfinished business of his life.
I just made up the part about him in a rowboat,
fishing being some of his best times.

In the rowboat, he tied a hook on a line,
fashioned a slab of plywood into an oar,
nailed, plugged, chopped and welded
all the materials of his backbreaking years.

This was great work for him and his face
was pinched with effort. Beads of sweat
glinted on his forehead as he gently laid
each of the items back into the water

from which they came, I imagine. The river
was grateful and in return rocked him
in its faithful current downstream
toward home,

which was a warm house filled with sisters
and all his old friends and Ma right there,
there, baking bread in the wood stove
from a recipe in her head.

Previously published in Linda Back McKay chapbook "The Cockeyed Precision of Time" and also in the 2007 St. Paul Almanac.

Poetry
by Richard Sederstrom

A New Kind of Night Again

Two storms in two days leave us a century
or millennium before electricity.
No light anywhere. Black water,
dark shores of the lake erase the ancient present.
We celebrate this dark beginning again
before the advent of the inevitable primordial blessing

of renewal, forbidden the rot-free polyethylene
human system fed for a mere century
on eons of black residue. We scour some residue
from lamp chimneys, trim wicks, remember,
almost, how to adjust for smokeless light.
We haul water up from the backbreaking lake.

*

We endure the inconvenience of slow machinery,
utterly trustworthy pain the modern neck,
and we enjoy the reward of the push and pull of it.
This yellow flame flicker of oil lamps
casts a softer reality than bottled light from bulbs,
ancestors winking back in respiring shadows.

This breeze-borne moving radiance
ridicules our industrious apostasy
toward Life, toward Nature, toward God.
In this welcome ancient gloaming, we read poems,
eyefilling corporeal messages, carboniferous,
inflammable in their ageless bright fuel.

We read a poem, maybe think, feel,
move to this languid flow of soft paper,
and if a poem rises to fill mind and moment,
we can turn down the flame. In that ancient light
we are born from the lines into the nurture,
the oneness of this reaffirming new night.

Poetry
by Marilyn Wolff

Acceptance

Winter settled into my bones this year

like an old dog circling
to make a bed
before a crackling fire,
finally curling up in the spot
just right for him.

Warm,

full-bellied,

satisfied with life.

Creative Nonfiction – Honorable Mention
by Julia Klebs
"Life's Cycle"

As I do every Saturday, I went to work on March 21, 2007. I expected it to be just another day.

Let me backtrack to September 2006. I work in a nursing home preparing meals for, on average, fifteen residents. My unit is usually filled to capacity, no empty beds. However, once in awhile one or more of those fifteen beds becomes empty, for various reasons. It doesn't stay that way for long, though.

Anyway, on this day in September, I was working and we had an empty bed. In the early afternoon, a new resident was moved in. As I normally do, I ventured down to the room after all the chaos had died down, mainly to introduce myself and to begin the ritual of getting acquainted.

I knocked on the open door and got a smart ass response: "The door's open, ain't it?" So I walked in, and there in front of me was a man who really didn't look like he belonged in a nursing home. He was tall, I could tell even though he was seated on the edge of the bed, and he was young. He didn't look to be a day over sixty. That's a rarity in my unit. And finally, he was smiling. Good sign.

I subtly checked the note I'd written on the palm of my hand before saying, "Hi, Leo."

"Well, ain't you just a purdy young thang?" he said. He wasn't from around here.

"Thanks," I said. "My name's Julie and I make the food here on the weekends." Same spiel I tell every new resident, even though half of them wouldn't remember who I was by their first meal there.

"Ah, good," he said. "Hot cooks make the best grub."

I had to ask, the drawl was beginning to bother me. "So where are you from, exactly?"

He laughed a little and said, "I've been 'round." He looked

me over again, then stuck out his hand to shake mine. When he saw his name scribbled on my skin, he smiled and said, "I think we'll get along just fine."

Over the next few weekends, I got to know Leo. He had advanced Parkinson's disease, and at times, it was apparent. Basically, he was no longer able to walk without the aid of a walker, and his tremors had become so bad that he couldn't perform simple tasks like preparing food or even feeding himself. However, he could disguise his symptoms well, and I assume that was how he avoided the move to the home for so long.

In one word, Leo was a flirt. He teased all the women who worked there, but he took a particular liking to me. I don't know why, but once in awhile someone really does. There's no rhyme or reason to it. Anyway, when I was working, he spent a good four hours of my eight-and-a-half hour shift in the kitchen or dining room, talking, clearing tables, sweeping the floors, and so on. They were good activities for him, and I didn't complain. Who would have a problem with someone doing their work for them?

One day in mid-December, Leo asked me a question that was really out of character for him. Usually our conversations focused on my love life or lack thereof, new recipes, stories from "back in the day," simple things like that. But that day he asked if I was afraid of dying. I told him I wasn't sure, then asked him if he was. He said he wasn't, then told me, "And it's a good thang too 'cause I reckon my time's comin'." Then he changed the subject, but I never forgot what he'd said.

One weekend in mid-January, I came to work and Leo's left arm was in a cast. He'd fallen in his bathroom and broken his wrist when he hit the floor. He proudly displayed the names that had been scrawled on the plaster and offered me a marker. For days, he showed everyone the cast, telling them, "She loves me, she really loves me. See the heart she drew by her name?"

I'd gotten used to this behavior. When I went to work on Saturday and made my daily trip down the hall to visit with my residents, I fully expected to see Leo standing in his doorway, waiting for me. But when I reached Leo's room, his bed was empty. His belongings were packed into boxes. His nameplate had been removed from the door. On rare occasions, people leave our nursing home to live with relatives, to return home, to go to another facility. However, I hadn't heard any such plans for Leo, and I'd only been gone five days. Plans don't get made and executed that quickly. Something had happened.

I went searching for a co-worker. I learned that during the week I'd been gone at school, Leo had suffered a series of mini-strokes. The strokes had rendered him unable to move the right side of his body or to speak properly. He'd been put on a respirator because he could no longer breathe on his own. He'd been reduced from endless chatter to shaky, sporadic written communication, from constant movement to almost complete immobility. He had been moved to a bed in the adjoining hospital, and things did not look good for him. Plans were being made to transfer him to another facility that was better equipped to care for him.

During my break on Saturday, I found my way to Leo's room and waited outside until the stream of visitors had slowed. I stood by his bed and waited until he opened his eyes. I didn't think he recognized me, but then he wrote on the legal pad he'd been given as I held it for him. It took him three tries to make the words legible. It must be more difficult than I can imagine, learning to write with the non-dominant hand so late in life. When he finally was satisfied with what he'd written, he dropped the marker and I turned the pad to read it. *Sorry you missed all the action.*

I'd told myself I wasn't going to cry. But I had to fight back tears as I told him, "That's just like you, always the smartass."

He smiled and I gave him back the marker, and held the pad again while he painstakingly drew the letters. *I'm going to miss you when they move me.*

I nodded. "I'll miss you too. But they've already gotten the paperwork submitted to transfer you to Duluth. Chances are they will get you moved sometime today." That's the way it always went when one of our residents was transferred. Three days or so if it was an urgent situation, a week or two if it wasn't, and Leo was definitely considered an "urgent situation."

He accidentally let the marker slip out of his fingers halfway through his next writing attempt, and I handed it back to him. I had to read the paper a couple of times to figure out what he'd written. *If you cry, it's going to make me cry too. And it ain't purdy when an old man cries. We tend to get ugly lookin'.*

I told him, "Didn't know it was possible for a man to get ugly looking just from a few tears. Hopefully today won't be my chance to find out."

Keep your chin up, he wrote then. I glanced at the clock and saw my half hour break was up, so I leaned over to give him a quick hug and a kiss on his forehead. "You better be decent to those nurses in Duluth," I said.

He took the marker back once more, and after he was done, I took the pad from him. *They won't ever measure up to you gals here. Thanks for all the good cookin', darling. Tell the rest of them I'll miss them too.* I tore off the marked-up sheets of paper and put them into my pocket before I left. I managed to hold back the tears until I was beyond the door.

Later that day, I heard Leo's family removing his belongings from his old room, and when they walked near the kitchen, I acted like I was busy. I walked back down to the hospital after my shift was over, and the room Leo had been in was empty. The next day, Sunday, the facility bus pulled up in front of the main doors, and I knew that on board was the resident who would be taking Leo's room. I watched out the window as the frail elderly man was lowered on the wheelchair lift to the ground, and as he was pushed into the building, I busied myself again. I didn't visit him.

Poetry

by Richard G. Hagen

Shoes

By the waters of Lake Calhoun I sat down
And removed my soccer shoes, knowingly
For the last time. Unlacing fifteen years.
Fun over; my feet needed to let out the pain.

So, aha, the pride, ten years later, when
Tying on softball shoes, back in shape.
Playing and running again, amid male camaraderie,
Planning the day my son would join us.

But legs give out, weight returns, cleats wear down.
My son, once on the roster, as a teammate, grew to a larger size,
Trading sport shoes for combat boots,
Sending me to the solace of soft spikes.

Now I juggle instruction with inconsistency,
Brief thrills with resignation, trudging along
Golf courses, unable to imagine quitting.
These shoes are just too darn comfortable.

Poetry

by Margaret Hasse

Rural Route 2, Box 4

Made of corrugated tin
The rural route mailbox is
A baby Quonset hut.
On a sturdy post saluting
With a red metal flag
The county postman
Who sits on the passenger side
And drives an old car
With his left hand.
Leaning out the window
On the right, he drops
The curved door
Of the mailbox on its hinge
Like an apron to a garage,
Removes out-going mail
That rests upright like ladders
To somewhere else,
Places inside a newspaper,
An advertising supplement,
And bills.
A handwritten letter
Has also found its way home
To this dirt road—
A birthday message
From a big brother
Traveling in his uniform
Who sends his love
And a lump wrapped in Kleenex:
A silver dollar for the child
To palm like an admission fee
To the wider world
She'll someday get to see.

Fiction – Honorable Mention

By Niomi Rohn Phillips

The Day the Nuns Wore Dresses

Bergdorf, North Dakota 1948

"Communists behind it," Johanna's dad said, scooping nails into a bag. "They're against religion. This anti-garb thing is just the beginning. They want to run the nuns out of our schools."

My best friend Johanna lived in an apartment above her dad's hardware store on Main Street. We were bored with the hot summer afternoon, and we were crouching in the stairway eavesdropping on the conversations below.

Lately, it seemed like everybody was talking about Communists. Like the depot agent might be one and Mike Placek who lived on the farm just outside of town and didn't go to mass at St. Mike's might be one. I finally worked up the courage to ask Mom about that St. Mike's thing since Daddy didn't go to mass either.

"Ignorance," she said. "Around here, if you aren't German and Catholic, you must be a Communist . . . and you don't have to repeat that!"

But what about this garb thing and the nuns? They were about the most important people in town, or at least at school and church, and that was the sum of a kid's life.

When the nuns swept down the street in their flowing black robes to buy groceries or pick up their mail, even the grownups stepped aside and muttered, "Good morning, Sister," or "Good afternoon, Sister."

When they came by Johanna's hardware store, we'd interrupt our hopscotch or push our wagons off the sidewalk to make way. If Johanna's dad was outside, they greeted him by his first name.

My dad didn't know the Sisters by name. In fact, my dad and the depot agent were the only Protestants in town. Maybe six farm kids in our school were Protestants. Grandma said the Protestants were the reason the Sisters might not be allowed to wear their habits anymore. That's what the anti-garb law meant. Mom and Grandma argued about it all summer.

"It's a public school," Mom said. "Some people don't want nuns teaching at all."

"Do they think the 'Catholic' will rub off on their kids if the nuns wear their habits? I suppose you are going to vote for it," Grandma said.

"It might seem ridiculous to you, Ma, but enough people petitioned to get it on a ballot, so we'd better take it seriously. We're just lucky they can teach here at all. I don't think there's another place in the country where nuns teach in public schools. This vote is making national news. Eloise Schmaltz has a cousin in Chicago, and she says the *Chicago Tribune* has been covering it all summer. They're saying the vote is dividing the State—Protestants against Catholics."

Mom argued with Uncle Nick about it too. He said he was "furious" that the government thought they could tell the nuns how to dress.

"There's a teacher shortage. They're better educated than most of the teachers around here. We should be glad they're willing to teach in this small town."

Mom came back with her public school speech and they ended that conversation with words I'd heard from him before, "Women shouldn't mess in politics."

The day of the vote was like a holiday only we didn't have to go to church. Every parking place was filled on Main Street. Kids ran all over while their parents stood in line to vote in the town hall.

People were standing around in Hager's grocery and the Farmer's Union and Johanna's hardware store and Johnny Schaan's Standard Oil on the corner. Nobody paid attention to us kids. We ran from one place to the other, reconnecting with farm friends we hadn't seen since the end of school.

Mom said she didn't even want to talk to Grandma the next day if the vote passed. It did—"with big margins," Daddy said. "There are only seventy-five nuns teaching in the state, but they can't wear their habits to school anymore."

All summer we heard the adults talking about the Sisters having to wear real people clothes, but they looked the same at mass on Sundays, sitting in the tenth row on the girls' side of the church.

We were hyper with curiosity and excitement on Monday morning, the first day of school. The fifth grade teacher was always Sister Mary Anastasia—old, wrinkled Sister Anastasia who especially hated boys and held a ready ruler to slap hands not working and tap heads not minding their own business. She had the kind of reputation that kept a kid awake half the night before the first day of school and made the oatmeal churn in your stomach at breakfast.

We were whispering and restless before the bell rang, waiting for Sister Mary Anastasia, but when the door opened into the fourth and fifth grade classroom, we were stunned into silence. The only sound was the meadow lark singing in the field outside when the stranger walked in. We didn't dare look at each other.

She had tight curled gray hair, like she'd taken the metal curlers out and not combed. It took us a few minutes to figure it out. A wig! We'd never seen anyone wear a wig except for a costume party.

She seemed fatter and shorter than the Sister Mary Anastasia we knew too. The black skirt and white blouse didn't disguise her shape like the robes of the habit. Her lips were tight, and she had an even crabbier face than usual, just daring us to snicker. As if we would. We'd be struck dead for sure. But without the swishing black robe and the big rosary hanging from the belt, and with that strange hair, she wasn't as scary as she'd been before. My stomach uncurled.

That first day we made a game of trying to get a look at all five nuns. What color hair do you think Sister Mary Ellen will have? What kind of dress will the principal, Sister Mary Dominic, wear?

Fifth graders weren't allowed in the basement sixth to eighth grade classrooms, or on the second floor high school. We had to make excuses to go to the outhouse hoping to get a glimpse or linger in the hallway on our way home for lunch.

Johanna and I peeked into the first and second grade room. Our favorite teacher, Sister Mary Ellen, had emerged like a butterfly from the stiff white face shell and black robe. We looked at each other with delight. Young and pretty. Like June Allyson. We would adore her.

Sister Mary Dominic tromped the halls as usual between her classes, making sure order was maintained, silence absolute, and no one loitered in the hallways on their way to the outhouses behind the school. She looked so strange with her head freed from the white band beneath the black veil and the bib under the chin. Her gray and black hair was pulled back in a bun thing, with her neck showing. We'd never seen her neck. And her blouse—there were gaps between the buttons. Breasts? Nuns have breasts?

She was even bigger in real clothes than in her habit, but I could feel a difference. She was still like a sentinel at the head of the stairs, but without her armor, daring us to show we noticed the change.

Johanna and I couldn't wait to get out of school to talk about the day. The mysterious life of nuns had always provided endless topics of interest, but this was new ground. Do you think they look in mirrors now? What do they wear in bed? How long is the hair underneath the wigs? Do you think they still shave their heads? How do the wigs stay on if their heads are shaved?

But they only needed wigs that first year. On the first day of sixth grade, we could see that the Sisters all had their own hair. Johanna and I exchanged furtive grins when Sister Mary Agatha pushed her soft brown curls back from her face and repeatedly ran her fingers through her hair. Vanity? A vain nun? Huh, not a saint. Just a woman after all.

Life was more confusing every year. Maybe all Protestants weren't Communists either.

(This fictive account from the point of view of a ten-year-old girl is based on fact. On July 2, 1948, an Anti-Garb Law passed in the state of North Dakota. A headline in the Chicago Tribune read "North Dakota Vote OKs Ban on Nun's Garb in Public Schools." The New York Times read "North Dakota Nuns to Adopt Civilian Dress in Order to Teach Under New State Curb.")

Poetry
by Kathleen Free

Dance With The Devil

She dances with the devil,
The devil of whirling emotion.
A storm of white satisfaction,
Trails of neon lights.

Cunning devil tickles her,
Until she begs for more.
She dances with the devil,
Until she cannot stop.

She loves the dance,
But she craves the devil.
She tries to balance
As she twirls.
Devil trips her,
Tips her.

She no longer sees
Shadows or light.
Slithering devil tricks her.
She's good, she thinks.

Her mind spins,
A wild dervish.
Blurring flights of delusion,
She knows she's right.

When she slows,
Sullen devil smirks.
She taps it on the nose,
Dances cheek to cheek.

I wait.
She thinks I do not see,
Yet I watch her dance.

Angels watch her dance.
They wait, too.
We wait.
We wait for years.

We wonder,
Without the devil,
Who might she be?

Poetry
by Annette Marie Hyder

the big melt

birds startle behind your eyes
your mouth holds a flood
that wants to wash out
foam over the cliffs
of what is between us

and that rush of water
has things in it
some ice still from the winter
some dead trees and detritus

my words are snares for your birds
my smile holds bridges
small ones, wooden ones
not anything
architecturally stunning

but my small wooden bridges
will make a way across
and my snares have taken your birds
so go ahead—say it.

Poetry

by Kathleen J. Pettit

Summer Road

On days filled with light, clear breezes
We walked the summer road that bordered the slough,
Bird book in one hand, "Wild Flowers" in the other.

Hidden in the wild grasses were extraordinary finds,
A splash of purple close to the ground,
Yellow marsh marigolds shaded by water willows,

A flash of a wing, scarlet on black velvet
Or yellow-headed black birds
Not yet cataloged in "Birds of North America."

We thirsted for the honey that nested in the red-bell
Columbine and the savory of wild sauerkraut,
Not knowing that someday

They would be as hard to come by
As a soft spring rain or
The sound of the slough-pumper's love song.

It was the camaraderie of discovery
That took us down the wagon-track road,
It was the naming of things that made it real.

Poetry
by Laura L. Hansen

Rain Lazy Day

Awake at 7 AM, the flannelled skies
Spread across the swift moving waters
Like fog, soft and dense, removing
Any chance of sun to penetrate
My slow moving mind

I sprawl on the bed, spend
Fifteen minutes, more,
Debating the choice of clothes
For the day, do nothing
But move my foot back under the covers

Nearly noon, I stare down at the keyboard
And will my hands to move, my thoughts
To clear, the skies to strip away the pall
Of gray, but under the cover of rain
My thoughts creep home

And slip under
Those two downy-thick comforters
Which have waited for me all day
On the rain lazy day unmade bed

Creative Nonfiction
by Anne Morgan

Spring Break

"Cows out," the old Finn said.

He left as abruptly as he spoke. Two days before, he'd unloaded twenty cows into a neighbor's pasture for the season. They were picking on freeze-dried weeds and stems, but we knew he'd feed hay bales until the grass started to grow.

I sighed. It was Sunday, five in the morning, but I didn't dare to go back to sleep. A farmer knows the difference between his cows and ours. And we were due for our annual spring break.

My husband scraped frost off the truck while I made coffee. We pulled out onto the county road and headed for the farm half a mile away. The approach of our driveway was riddled with hoof prints.

"I wonder where they got out." Dewane ground out a cigarette in the ash tray, took off his stocking cap, and rubbed the windshield.

Holding my breath, I pressed my forehead into the passenger window. Ghostly streamers fogged the ditch. "I don't see them," I said.

He drove slowly past the barn. The garden. Our son's driveway.

One mile.

Two.

"I don't see them," I said. "Think they're out?"

"They could be down the section road." He turned around and backtracked toward the barn.

Charmin, the old Palomino who thinks she is a cow, and the new rental bull, who may never comprehend that the world extends beyond the confines of a fence, stood stoically in the cow yard. Sixty-odd cows and calves milled outside. Some yanked jagged mouthfuls of winter-green hay from the big round bales we had saved back in case of a late spring. Two yearling steers, always more eager to play than eat, bunted heads. Four calves with twitching tails crowded around the open barn door as six laying hens emerged, escorted by the big red rooster.

The lead cow stopped scratching her chin on the hay spike on the back of the tractor. On her silent mark, the older cows broke into a crazed, cavorting dance. Hind heels high in the air, they gyrated north, past us, and past the compost piles. Eyeing us warily, the calves hung back, then followed.

I jumped out of the truck. Dewane shifted into 4-wheel low and plowed through a series of treacherous, muddy, spring-thaw puddles. He reached the gate to the garden seconds before the lead cow.

Bovine brains surely ruminated on defeat as I opened the right gate, the one into the cow yard. I backed up and pointed the way like an ambulatory scarecrow.

One mama, closest to me, led her small, black calf into the cow yard. The newborn lowered its head, latched onto a front teat, and resumed its nursing.

The lead cow, mottled gray and white, charged past the opening and darted through a narrow, brush-choked gap between the garden fence and the tin-sided loafing shed.

The rest of the herd debated and followed.

We parked near the south side of the cow yard and heard the rhythmic snap of broken electric fence wire. Parallel strands had snaked through the hay bales, one marking the current feed line, the second, a back-up. White fiberglass rods with bright yellow insulators jutted at odd angles of mute witness.

Cows and calves stood behind us, watching as we untwisted wire. We spliced and re-stretched. They called to the bull, who answered with a high-pitched, effeminate low. He had no idea how —or why—they got out.

The lead cow sauntered off into the woods. By twos and threes, the herd followed.

"Get in," Dewane yelled. "The gate by Joe's is open."

He accelerated onto the highway, whizzed past the garden, and turned sharp into our son Joe's driveway. Around the shop, down the hill. We bounced over old gopher mounds until we reached the east edge of the woods, and hooked up the fence before the cows appeared.

"That'll stop them," I offered, retrieving my coffee cup from under my seat.

"Nope. They can circle around the slough and run out onto the fields."

We drove out our son's driveway and looped back onto the farm. They had circled around the slough.

This was the first opportunity we'd had to inspect our fences for deer damage; the snow had just retreated off the tree-lined lanes. We patched the most obvious holes and returned to the truck.

Soon, the lead cow and her attendants charged up. Unaccustomed to exertion after a long winter of standing, they breathed heavily. They lined up along the fence and looked at us expectantly.

The lead cow, with the hard, skyward horns, mooed her disappointment. She had found nothing worth eating.

Dewane reminded her of the alfalfa grass hay bales in the cow yard. He mentioned their decision to pass the correct, open gate in favor of the brush and the woods.

From off in the distance, several cows seconded her sentiment.

The mooing escalated into a ragged duet that lasted as long as a three verse hymn.

Dewane lit another cigarette.

The strains of the final 'Amen' faded away.

They stomped their hooves and snorted.

Finally, I'd had enough. I wanted a fresh, hot cup of tea. CBS Sunday morning could still be on. "Grain," I snapped. "Let's just give them some grain, get them back in and be done."

The cows gazed intently as Dewane poured mounds of grain on the driest spots in the cow yard.

"Let them in," he called.

I opened the south gate, hoisted the fifty-pound burlap sack up on my shoulder and trudged out of the way.

The lead cow and her lieutenants made a beeline for the grain. The calves hung back.

"Dump your bag over there." Dewane pointed at the fence line by the stock tank. I dribbled out a line of grain under the bottom bar of the green metal stock panel until my sack was empty. Then I climbed over the fence and circled around behind the calves. Dewane came around the other way and we herded in the hesitant stragglers.

"Can't really blame them," he said after we tested the electric charge in the wires that again snaked through the feed line of hay bales. "They've been stuck in the cow yard for months. It's muddy and the snow's gone."

"What did they expect to find?" I grumbled. "Magical patches of green grass?"

He shrugged. "You'd want to look."

"Think they've gotten it out of their system?"

"Maybe, maybe not. They know other cows are out on pasture."

Poetry

by Kathy Herzog

Running From Sunday

I think of years gone by—
Colorful Sunday ads
Rattling catalog pages
Circling sweaters hoped for

Battery operated clock
like a rain gauge
collects drips
of the day

Lingering
in the space
after slipping from Sunday best,
more lemon pie, and 60 Minutes

Where have Sundays gone?
Why am I compelled
to keep moving
even on the day of dreams?

Poetry

by C. Mannheim

Nightfall on a Crowded Porch

Languid shadows stretch and yawn
swallowing up summer hues

The hint of cool that rides on heavy air now
tarnishes the golden shimmer of twitching leaves;
as reds' radiant glow trails after sun's retreat
their tempo slows

Cyans, blues leach out of sky and trees,
bridged now by growing, graying unity

Avian vespers first amplify, then fade
as a half-moon ignites in deepening skies

Scents of bloom, whispering foliage
and the distant giggles of child's play
alone are left to texture the night

before whining, overworked A/Cs,
the thudding pulse of passing bass,
and roaring stream of rushing cars
crowd the dark sweet solitude.

Poetry
by Harold Huber

The Creek

It whispers as it weaves along
Tiptoeing pace but toeless
A meandering, sleepwalkish path
Edged with cattails and reeds

One yard wide where I'm standing
Less where it curves to the east
Knee deep at most, I imagine
Ankle depth, more likely

Water-cress tracts, mosaics of shell
Giraffe spots dotting the route
Sun curls on swift sliding surface
Spotlighted patterns below

Rocks turned to mossy islands
Whirlpools in their wake
Wee darting beasties cavort
Sticklebacks smack their lips

Chilled in December—stilled
Sparkling views frosted over
Creek dances stopped for the season
Awaiting the fiddles of Spring

Slender white road paved with snowflakes
Do currents still flow underneath?
Planning some April surprises
For daydreaming fans such as I?

Might you alter the well worn pathway?
Veer off to the west? Head north?
Split up into skinny creeklets?
Make loops as you slither by?

Perhaps I'm being too nosey
Perhaps you have secrets to keep
Perhaps you're fed up with perhapses
I'll stop now and just watch you sleep

Poetry
by Christopher Schmitz

Granite

A solitary stone I am.
Earth hardened, speckled pigment.
I sit.
Glistening from the wetness;
It's raining.
Ripe green grass grows up around me,
Beaten down now by the downpour.
Pale moonlight illuminates the scene,
Captured, as an image embossed in silver.
The moon peeks between the fat
Coal clouds and the phantom black sky.
The rain comes down.
The grass and cattails sway under
The weight of the precipitation.
The drops slowly erode me
Over the course of all these years.
Earth hardened and weather softened:
I sit.
It never stops falling.
Ironically, forged in fire:
I am igneous—
Heat crafted by chaos and flame
Yet happily I succumb to the sky's
Gentle probing and molding by the
Never ending drizzle.

Poetry

by Anja Kuehne-Welsh

Being Scandinavian

Being Scandinavian, I do not expect my grandmother
to understand me when I tell her about my therapy
or how I cry when I imagine her gone.

My husband talks about dahl and gorgonzola and green chilies
over potatoes and fish at a family dinner,
and no one says anything.

As a child I wore a kirtle and kerchief to camp.
I learned to pronounce words with double vowels, and
was given a Finnish name although I already had one.

There are many secrets buried between the northern pines.
I watch the snow drifting across the field with a mind of its own
and wonder if my grandfather did the same.

The churches here are white and the cemeteries are small.
Little curved stones of different sizes gather moss
and are still readable.

At our family dinners, the sun shines through the windows
crisp and clear and silent.
We all sit in the same chairs every time.

And lately, Grandma spouts about how great it once was.
She goes on about the farm, the food,
and the simplicity.

You can't get a word in.
So I sit back, feed my daughter a piece of toast,
and say nothing.

Fiction
by LuAnne White

The Sales Pitch

I had both doors of the store open that day. It was so hot. The industrial sized fan in the window wasn't doing much. The noise whuffled through my head, blowing any thoughts of work from my mind. The chocolate candy was safely stashed in the milk and beer coolers so it wouldn't melt. Not much business today. Everyone was in the lake or on their way there. They weren't buying anything. I was toying with the idea of restocking some of the shelves or dusting when Timothy, the one-pizza-a-month man, ambled in. I just ignored the large black dog that wandered in after him and went right on through and out the back.

"Sure is hot today. Got a cold one in the fridge?" I eyed him a moment before replying. He didn't appear to be drunk but he knew better than to ask that when he was sober.

"Tim, you know I only sell it by the case. I thought you only drank with the guys at the tavern nowadays."

"Well, I'm on my own this week. Wife is visiting the daughter. So the guys are coming for poker later. I'll have a case of that Bud Light and some goodies."

I pulled his case of beer from the cooler and asked him what kind of treats. He wasn't quite sure. I recognized the signs. Hunger. I also remembered that he didn't know how to cook. The last time his wife went away, he had take-out every meal including breakfast. I gathered up chips of various kinds, some dips, and some summer sausage. I gave him a piece of the cheese I was having for lunch as I passed by my desk.

"Are you calling for pizza for supper, too? Or are they coming later than that?"

"Oh, hell. I told them to come for dinner but you know the pizza place that delivered out this far has shut down. Damned inconvenient of them. I hate your frozen pizzas and can never get them cooked right anyway. I wish I could cook something myself. I'm so tired of the woman telling me what an idiot I am spending so much money on take-out every time she leaves. It's downright irritating." He took out his cigarettes and put one in his mouth, reaching for his lighter.

"Not in here, Tim." He mumbled something incoherent from behind the cigarette.

"Why not serve them something besides pizza? I'm sure you could find something else in here instead."

"I still can't cook!"

"Have you ever tried to?" I challenged.

"Uh, well, I guess not really. I tried to cook some stew once. Burnt it and ruined the pan. That's about it. I can make tomato soup from a can. But I can't give that to the guys. Pete had this really cool spread at his place last time. Sometimes I hate poker night. Don't know why I play anyhow. I hardly ever win either." He ran his sunburned hand over his close-cropped white hair. You could see the scalp through it—red like his hands.

"Maybe you play for company and fun? I'll help you make a stew that is simple and quick. You won't have to pay attention for more than twenty minutes. Can you stay in the kitchen and tend a pot for twenty minutes, Tim?"

"Yeah, I guess so. What kind of stew can you make like that?"

"We had it every Wednesday night while I was growing up. Dad had to go to Reserve classes that night and Mom made this stew and dumplings. You don't even need a mixing bowl for the dumplings." I got out some paper from under the cash register and started writing the recipe down.

"Go get this stuff as I read it off: Bisquick, two cans of stewed tomatoes, two cans of Dinty Moore stew, 1 quart of milk, two cans of mushrooms. Do you like green beans and corn in your stews or do you like it more basic?" He brought a can of beans and a can of com to the counter in answer. I finished writing the recipe and carefully went over it with him.

"Put all the ingredients into a large pot with a cover and cook on medium until it starts to boil. While that's going on, you make your dumplings in the now empty stew can. Directions are on the box; follow them exactly! Oh, and don't forget to add either a glass of red wine or a glass of beer to the stew before you add the dumplings."

He was grinning as he took the groceries out. If I could get all the men whose wives took vacations without them to cook and therefore buy groceries, I'd make a little more cash!

Next day Timothy came back with his hang-dog expression on. I figured he goofed up the recipe, though I couldn't see how he could do that.

"Got another recipe like that? Thought I'd have my golfing buddies in tomorrow."

Poetry
by Connie Claire Szarka

The Hunt

I follow Vic in waders through the woods to Slaughter Slough.
An autumn sun filters down on us
through sugar maples, red oaks, and butternuts.

Silent, we set out decoys, then wait, crouched among the reeds.
If I were a Mallard, I'd swoop in to the sound of Vic's call
chattering, clucking away the quiet.

A flock keys in from the north
and circles above our painted ducks.
One will fall—I feel it in my young bones.

The butt of my Ithaca
tight to shoulder,
I draw a bead and squeeze the trigger.

Wings freeze, then fold in mid-flight.
Feathers ajumble, the collapsed bird plunges
into Slaughter Slough.

I wade through marsh and muck
to retrieve my first kill—a big drake, still warm,
his emerald head dangling, glinting in the sunshine.

On solid ground,
Ithaca high above my head, I caw
and dance around in clumsy circles.

Vic, stern-faced, steps into my ring,
takes away my shotgun.
"I never taught you to be a crow," he says.

Poetry
by David Henke

A Sestina on Solitude

My dice, my bobbleheads, my dashboard shrines,
shrink with the heat. The asphalt wavers like a prayer
evaporating in the sun. This unending road
rolls away. The pistons in the engine pump a river
of gasoline, and the car's rumbling is the noisy story
of America. There are fifty-three miles

until the next rest stop. My imagination wanders for miles;
I dream of desert caravans, of Saharan shrines,
of camels, silk, men with windblown robes. Their story
is my story; all of our travels are a prayer
issued to the god of wanderlust. We are rivers
of humanity, splayed out like veins on roads.

You're asleep in the passenger seat, and I think: The road,
the towns, all of these crow-filled fields, these miles,
are nothing but landmarks for our love. Our lives a river
that sinks into itself, these hours together a shrine
filled with joyful, idle talk. Our intimacy a prayer.
We are lovers from all the old stories.

Men sitting in halls lit with singing will tell our story
for generations. We will be the model, our love the road
map that all others follow. My tires sing a prayer
to you as I eat away the miles.
An hour later I stop at a gas station, a shrine
to Krispy Kremes and porno mags. A river

of loneliness runs from this place. Gas spills in rivers
onto the dark cement. The old truckers spin stories
and sip coffee. Their slow speech is a shrine
to weary hours spent listening to late night radio, on roads
that lead them to Hayward, Menahga, Ponemah, towns that are miles
away from their families, girlfriends, children. I need a prayer

here; while you, sleeping in the sideseat, are blissful like a prayer.
I'm glad that you don't see the solitude, a river
that stretches in the faces of these men for miles.
I walk back to the car, where you lie lost in the stories
of your dreams. Each step is punctuated by the hope that our roads
don't diverge, that we never need to build, for separation, a shrine.

That we, a shrine, aren't worn down by the miles.
That you, the road that I follow, let your story
wind, river-like, into my love, and rise like a prayer.

Creative Nonfiction
by Sharon Ness

The Last Stitch

I opened the dusty cedar chest searching for photos of my fortieth class reunion. I found a strange swatch of orange at the bottom of the chest. I hugged this material close to me, sniffing for scents of Mama's kitchen. Oh, Mama, I remember!

Twenty four of us graduated in 1963. We planned a class trip to Duluth. We were required to dress up. The girls wore dresses and nylons. The boys wore dress pants, shirts, and ties. None of us had been very far from home. My experience eating out was limited to potluck church suppers, school fund raisers, and the one and only ice cream soda fountain in town. Occasionally my family took me to a buffet in a nearby town. Before we left on the trip, my home economics teacher taught all of us proper manners and how to order from a complicated menu.

Since I needed to dress appropriately in Duluth, Mama bought orange and white gingham material for sewing a dress. The pattern had a three yard gathered skirt with cross stitch decorations at the bottom. The intricate cross stitch design was six inches wide. My sister volunteered to do the cross stitching.

Just a few days before the trip, the dress arrived in the mail without the cross stitching. My sister ran out of time. With Mama's chores at home and community activities, I could not imagine her finishing the dress before we left on our trip.

I pouted for days believing that I wouldn't have anything new to wear. The night before the trip, I went to bed early. Between the tears and worrying about missing the bus at 6 a.m. the next morning, I didn't sleep much. It seemed like I had just fallen asleep when Mama called, "Sharon, it's time to get up."

Pulling back the curtain at the bottom of the stairwell, I saw Mama sitting in her chair taking the very last cross stitch on my dress. She had stayed up all night sewing. I gave Mama a hug. "You worked all night knowing that you are substituting for our teacher today who will chaperon our class trip."

I wore the dress for several years before leaving it in Mama's closet. After I married and moved away, Mama sent me a smock to wear during my pregnancy. She found that long forgotten dress from my high school days and used the bottom three yards for a smock. I wore it through two pregnancies before storing it in the attic.

Years later, a package arrived on my birthday from Mama. I pulled out an orange and white gingham material with brown cross-stitching. What a surprise. She found one more way to use the dress—the one she stitched all night to finish. Now the apron she made from that same material lies in my cedar chest with memories of Mama biting off the thread as she completed that last stitch, just for me.

Poetry
by Richard Carr

Uncle Mike

A boy in bed, I listened to the clank
of glasses in the kitchen through the wall.
The men sat 'round the table late and drank.
"We'll make the oath on his mother's good shawl:
Let none forget our Mike!"—But down the hall,
the women spoke against a heathen wake,
and in their beds, owl-eyed, despised the gall
of them who'd happily sing "Nell Flaherty's Drake"
on burial eve. Someday I too would slake
my grief in the old family way and, rank
with whiskey, claim the dregs, cursing the snake
that lets our loved ones die. And then I'd thank
my uncle Mike: "That night I learned to bawl—
to sing loud, boys, and damn them down the hall."

Poetry

by David Henke

In Lieu of Ice Fishing

One night we dropped the tackle and the line
in a corner of the ice house, and drank
whiskey, played hold 'em poker and bullshit.
Winter is a privacy, so we told

all the crude jokes, and jumped in snow naked.
We filled silence with wild, made-up stories,
exaggerated accounts, arguments,
kisses, truth or dare. This is the joy

of being young; we smiths can architect
our lives, fill empty bodies with dancing
and frenzied late nights; it seems our lives are
a loaded gun, cocked to go off, and fire.

Poetry
by Charmaine Donovan

Stair-Struck

I used to count stairs as a kid.
In our house, fifteen from the first to second floor.
Five from the walk to our front door.
I counted silently, the way other kids
tried not to step on sidewalk or tile cracks.
I did it without meaning to, like breathing.

Today stairs startle me.
When I see escalators or elevators, I cry.
I smell smoke and fuel. Singed hair and flesh.
The shuffled sound of shoe soles on stairs.
An uneven cadence. Groans and creaks.
Sometimes people, sometimes buildings,
falling away beside me, below me.
I avoid gray or black items,
haven't barbecued since September.

Stairs saved my life.
Stairs saved hundreds of lives.

I love them, yet cannot bear being close to them.
I appreciate where they led me:
from pinnacle of death and crushing noise
to silent smoking skies,
away from the crime scene.

Away from the smudged horror on faces
that visit me in smoldering dreams.
Dreams of stairways that stop or crumble.
Stairways that melt right up my legs.
I fold into them. I wake up screaming.
My bed sheets are damp and cool.
I listen in the bedroom dark
as my lungs subside.
I groan in gratitude. In guilt.
I groan in stupid spirit,
cry out to a failing creator,
too sky-high for me to reach right now.

Stairs connect me to heaven and hell.
I went down, you see.
It was the only way out.
Up was an inferno.
Down was cool, almost calm.

Now I burrow down like a mole
in the hole of my own pain.
Murky as it may be,
I tolerate darkness far better
than blazing, burning light.

Fiction – Honorable Mention

by Susan Wolter Nettell

History Stains

Whomp.

Lily McKinzie slammed the reinforced metal door to her apartment with a back kick of her foot. That felt good. She juggled the cardboard box she carried to one side and slipped off her shoes, leaving them in a jumbled pile on the rug. She walked through the kitchen and set the box on the table, slipped off her coat and dropped it over the back of a chair. The sloppiness was deliberate, a childish gesture of silent defiance.

"Mom, I don't want to be perfect," had been an adolescent battle cry for Lily, an only child who had come late in her parents' marriage.

Her mother, Ester McKinzie, kept an immaculate house, all drawers and closets were organized, and she was never late for an appointment. Lily squeezed toothpaste in the middle of the tube, stacked mismatched plates in the same pile, and even let things lay on the floor where they had been dropped.

This weekend the skirmish had been over the cardboard box sitting on her table—a win, but one that left Lily with emotional residue.

Lily picked up the box and carried it over to her sofa. She set it down, clicked on lamps to dispel the encroaching evening shadows, and plopped down on the sofa.

Lily opened the flaps. Jumbled together inside the box were stacks of photographs. She breathed in deeply: yellowed paper, ink, a hint of dry leather. The photos had once belonged to her Grandmother Lucinda. After Grandma Lucinda died, Ester took the box and promptly consigned it to an old leather trunk in the basement, where it had stayed until today.

Lily gently lifted a stack of photographs from the box and set them on her lap. She smiled. Yes. These were perfect. Her shoulders relaxed. She had been right to push to get the box.

The top black and white photograph was of her grandmother's house, a white two-story box with a roof. Behind the house, trees, thick and mature, staked a claim to having been there first. In front, the trees had been cleared, and plowed acreage nearly met the front door. A narrow dirt road snaked in from the right side of the picture.

Her Uncle Rob and Aunt Faye lived there now. The house was no longer white, and machinery crowded the yard. A large patio with a barbeque grill reached out from the front of the house and gathered everyone together in the summer. Lily loved her Uncle Rob's house and family, but this old photo captured the past.

Lily was enrolled at the University of Minnesota in the Graduate Program in History. Her thesis explored how agriculture had historically impacted not only the lifestyle, but the personality, appearance, and philosophy of rural Minnesota families.

Lily had spent the past weekend interviewing and observing her own rural Minnesota family.

Uncle Rob's jeans sported a streak of axel grease and his pickup box carried an assortment of tools, twine, and oil. Her dad's deeply tanned hands and scarred knuckles spoke loudly to Lily, as did his gruff tone, a camouflage for the emotional stake in farming: the hope in spring planting, the jubilation of fall harvest, and the worry in between.

Aunt Faye was practical. Vacations and weddings had to be scheduled around seeding and harvest. And there was always the uncertainty. You never knew what the season would bring: too much rain, not enough rain, crop disease, or low prices at the elevator.

"The year we built the new addition on the barn, we had just got the 2x4 walls up and it hailed so hard the entire crop was pounded into the ground in fifteen minutes." Aunt Faye shook her head. "It's hard to start something costly like that without wondering if you are spending money you don't have."

"Mom, do you like farming?" Lily asked, leaning against the kitchen counter as her mother peeled carrots.

Ester shrugged, the gesture inelegant. "Farming's fine."

Ester McKinzie was a tall woman, with a thinness that never filled out her large, bony joints. She lacked the grace of wheat heads bobbing in the wind, and more closely resembled a cultivator, practical, spare, and tough. Ester set down the vegetable peeler and reached for a paring knife.

"Did you ever wish for something different?"

Ester's smile faded and she stared at a far corner of the counter for a moment. She shook her head and started chopping carrots with a rhythmic snick, snick, snick of the knife.

"No Lily, there's no use wishing for something you can't change."

Lily slowly sifted through the stack of photographs, carefully placing them in a pile next to her. She paused at a family photo in front of a black car. A young Ester in a print dress stood next to Grandpa Henry, fashionably topped in a black bowler hat. Grandma Lucinda, her hair dark and back still straight, was holding a baby in her arms. The baby was Lily's aunt, but she had died very young and Lily was sorry to realize she couldn't even recall her aunt's name. The picture had been taken several years before the birth of Uncle Rob.

The next photo of an apple orchard and apple pickers in large floppy hats delighted Lily. Her building excitement softened the sharp corners of her irritation.

"What's the point of keeping things if they just sit in a trunk and no one looks at them?" Lily asked her mother.

"That stuff needs to be sorted," Ester said as she poured batter into a greased pan. She was baking bars for a benefit auction; a neighbor had been diagnosed with stomach cancer.

"Let me sort it," Lily suggested.

"No."

"But Mom, why?" Lily asked, feeling the familiar pinch of her mother's control.

"It's my responsibility." The cake pan scraped across the oven rack as Ester slid it inside.

"I can handle it."

"That old junk can't help you." Ester set the timer on the oven and left the room.

Lily wanted to scream. Or maybe throw something. Or take it anyway. Her mother would never know. No one ever opened the trunk. She squashed the thought with a few years of earned maturity and enlisted her father's help.

Sid McKinzie was an easy-going man, as rounded from too many slices of buttered bread as his wife was spare. He preferred to leave such matters to Ester's discretion, but Lily played her trump card.

"Dad, I need it for my graduate program."

Sid had never gone beyond high school. The University, and especially the Graduate Program, were bestowed the greatest respect.

"Ester, let her have the old pictures."

Ester shook her head. "I need to sort them."

"Let go, Mom," Lily said, chopping the words short. "You can't control everything."

Ester's lips pinched together.

Ring. At the sound of the telephone, Ester stood.

"Ester, you're being unreasonable." Lily's head turned at her father's unusually harsh words.

Ester's spine stiffened.

"Well, it's true," Sid continued. "Let Lily look. That's her family history, too."

Ring.

"History is for people with too much time on their hands," Ester replied.

Lily's muscles tensed. "Does that mean me?"

Ester sighed and shook her head. "No."

Ring.

"I have to get the phone."

Lily closed her eyes and gritted her teeth. It would

never occur to her mother to just let the phone ring.

"Hello?" Ester immediately began to talk about the items expected at the benefit auction.

Sid jerked his head in the direction of the basement and said softly, "Go ahead. I'll talk to her."

Lily left shortly thereafter, tightly gripping the steering wheel, and her frustration at her mother's stubborn nature, on the two hour drive back to St. Paul.

Lily lifted out another stack of photos. The top photo was a long, horizontal picture of a threshing crew: oxen, horses, thresher, separator, and a large assortment of people, men and boys by the machines, women and small children in front. Lily's smile widened as she examined the clothing and hats. Agriculture affected everything and everyone.

A folded piece of yellowed paper was in the stack, worn at the crease and easily identifiable as newsprint. Lily carefully opened the article and read.

Tragic Accident Kills Area Youngster

In a tragic accident last Monday, three-year old Lillian Hoffman, daughter of Henry and Lucinda Hoffman, fell to her death on the family's staircase. The child's mother and older sister, Ester, were home at the time, but they were unable to bring the child back from heaven's gate.

Reverend Richard Stevens offered the family this consolation, "Her Lord called her to His Kingdom. We can be thankful she went to Him without suffering here on this troubled earth."

The funeral will be held on Friday at 4:00 at Banner Methodist Church. Interment will follow immediately after the service in the adjacent church cemetery. All are welcome to attend.

The cause of the accident was a rag doll tragically left on the stairs by the older sister.

Poetry

by Karsten Piper

Across North Castle Street

At that door, a girl
leans in to the glass,
wipes away raindrops.
Her hand is a branch
against the red door,
the only movement,
the only color.
Yet no one says, *I am here—*
no ones says, *Not here*
—says to her, *Later*.
The cobbles spill with water.
Her hair hangs lank
and dripping as the rain,
as the rain ploughs
the fog of her calling.
At no one's answer,
she stands narrow
as an aspen bough
and peers again.

Poetry

by Frances Ann Crowley

After Four Generations

If the old house could spill its guts,
the stone foundation would laugh about
the time that bull snake tried to get back out,
but the strong rancher pulling on her tail,
his foot against the wall, stopped her.

Of course, the cold storage room would tattle
on the hired men who would sneak down
to steal jars of preserved peaches and pickles,
because the young wife didn't cook enough
to keep a bird alive.

The kitchen window would tell of the time
she shoved his head through it—
the head being attached to a drunk
who was loaded, waving a gun (unloaded)
in her face while she was grinding
the coffee for breakfast.

The oak, claw foot dining table
would say that a little dirt under your nails
isn't necessarily a bad thing.
While the upright grand in the corner
would play Mozart, *Chopsticks*
and *Home on the Range*.

Upstairs, the bottom drawer of the built-in chest
would open and out would fly the medals,
patches and pins of the WWII Navy pilot
who died while hunting coyotes out of an airplane.
The high school paper cradling his poetry would cry.

And, recalling the teenagers on the way home
from a movie and their car crashing into a bridge
where two were killed, the brass bed would point
to the hollow in the mattress made by a
heavy heart, lying there for days and days,
speaking to no one.

Poetry
by Lane Rosenthal

07.07.2005

We bury my neighbor the same day
the bombs explode in the London Underground.
She killed herself July fourth, slowly,
one cigarette at a time, until the malignancy
hidden in her lungs, discernible only
through a throaty voice and a cough
so violent it made you look away
fearing the fear in her eyes, finally
took hold, finding her bones and brain
hospitable hosts. By the time the gravediggers
broke ground, upturning the fragrant black soil,
the bombs had exploded—one, two three—and
news circled the globe like smoky entrails.

I sit outside a bakery with a catchy name
sipping coffee in the sunlight of a shamefully
bright day, the kind that people want to bottle up,
the better to savor some future, frigid day.
Only, who would unleash the horror again?
At the curb in front of where I sit
a woman dressed head to toe in neon pink emerges
from a Porsche Carera convertible and glides,
audacious, oblivious, on shiny-sandaled, painted-toe feet,
past me.

At a school down the street a ten-year-old boy,
my son, sits in an American Red Cross Babysitting class
learning how to behave in an emergency:
when to call the parents, when to call 9-1-1; but not
what to do when a bomb explodes in your face
on an ordinary midsummer's day.

Poetry

by Susan Niemela Vollmer

Wind Generators

Across the western prairie
Sprouting along the ridge

A flock of wind generators
Languidly wave their graceful arms

They could be prehistoric creatures
Herding peacefully together

Or beings with futuristic semaphores
Sending and receiving messages

Communicating with distant galaxies
Stirred by breezes past and future

Creative Nonfiction
by Traci Nigon

Perfect Stranger

I am clunky jewelry that I never wear. I'm fast-food wrappers strewn throughout a car from a road trip to visit my very best friend, eight hours away. I'm a stale answering machine, unused and empty.

Flashing lights signal a message, and I am those too. I'm a snooze button, repetitious, sometimes too soft. I'm a Dean's List letter stuck to the wall, a dirty pan that is cleaned only when needed for use, and the key that broke off my laptop last year. I can be a few shots of vodka, a beer, a glass of milk, a glass of water; my mood dictates the beverage of choice. Some days I'm a treadmill or elliptical, while others I stay in pajamas and rarely leave my bed.

My soul comes from Rocky Mountains and snow and splendidly green trees; my attitude comes from crazed taxis and skylines, Hong Kong crowds and neon lights; my humility comes from rows of breadbasket corn waving like a concert audience in the pale blue sky. The stars are always there, changing with the seasons and geography and weather, but still fundamentally the same. I have yet to determine my sky.

I could be a sleek black dress, but more often than not, I am jeans and a sweatshirt—sometimes with makeup. On exceptional days, I am pinstriped pants and liquid eyeliner, and on funky days, I'm a black sweatshirt and dark mascara and a green boy's hat. I'm a pair of cute three-dollar black boots that I found in the kids' section at Wal-Mart.

I grew from country twang into bubble-gum pop, moved on to bass-filled rap, then angelic choir harmonies, then alternative rock. I revert back to each of these in turn, but what really strikes a chord in me is basic piano and guitar. I can add my voice to any melody, whether spoken or played, or sit quietly and feel what the music is meant to say. I'm an iPod, but only because it was a gift.

There I am, a blank sheet of paper, a pen poised and ready

with nothing to push it into action. And over there, a to-do list with random scribbles haphazardly slashed out. I am a dichotomy, an oxymoron, and sometimes just a moron. I'm a lover of knowledge and a lack thereof.

My room holds a Bible, though I'm not sure where. A tattoo on my back is a cross with a rose snaking around it. I have books on religion, I have visited Buddhist and Taoist temples, and I have seen scrolls of the Torah. I agree with Gandhi, who said that a friendly study of world religions is a sacred duty, yet am so wrapped up in current moments that many studies never manifest into reality. I have gone to church roughly fifty out of fifty-two weeks every year. Some days I struggle and some days I'm an atheist, but other days my convictions are defended with absolute certainty.

I am drunken phone messages at three in the morning, and I am a quiet night at home with hot chocolate and a good movie—as long as there's a blanket and a buddy to cuddle. I am *The Chipmunk Adventure* and *Casablanca* and *V for Vendetta* wrapped into one. Three-fourths of boys kissed were single cases of drunken lust, and the fourth was a two-year tumultuous relationship of learning and real, honest love. I am a single girl out on the town with no desire for a one-night stand. I have been in love but never made it. I am two instances of smoking pot, drunken instances of smoking cigarettes, and limitless instances of attending class, going to meetings, and achieving, whether over or under.

Smiles and sunshine surround me, but crabby days and jealousy bubble below the brim. I am a rubber band that can snap at people when stretched, and I am tears streaming in solitary darkness or emotional arguments. I am a peacemaker and an instigator. I took self-defense but can be confrontational. I was a Judo player for one semester and am a Judo student every time I'm around my guy friends. I am powerful, playful, passive, persuasive, perverted, pure. I am hurt, but I can heal the heart.

I am hours of road trips with nothing but a car, a few pairs of unfolded clothes, cheap food, and a best friend or two. I am a double-decker bus on the left side of the road or an airline flight scrunched next to a stranger. I'm not a train, but I would like to be. I have no sense of internal direction but have found myself in places of awe. Beaches or caves or forests can intrigue my mind at any moment. I am sunsets and sunrises, midnight blue and radiant afternoon sun. I chase the stars. I stand on a cruise boat's edge with arms stretched like Rose; I wander the Mongolian desert and see how people could easily have gotten lost. I wonder about the footprints that lead nowhere. And I head home again and am the small-town girl who belongs to neither city life nor country life, though I sometimes feel maybe my peace of mind depends on both and everything in between.

I am an all-nighter after playing too hard. I'm an all-weekend partier after working too hard. I am hours of concentration and moments of flight. I have the inquisitive mind of a detective and the ambition of a floppy mop. I am dreams. Someday potential will be reached, but it is not today, and it is always today to me.

I am the sum of experience but not yet a full equation. I am either versatile or a hypocrite or both. I am limitless; I'm the perfect stranger that could change your life.

Poetry

by Patricia Conner

Lovers and Friends

Lovers, wrapped around their longing,
have no use for strangers;
they gaze only into each other's eyes
and give themselves completely to assays
of reciprocity. They must acquire
a fair return on their investment.

Friends stand side by side and stare
at a common vision, observing
through a shared lens. Self is lost.
Beyond is all. Hands joined, they may
climb up or march together, carry protest
signs, support each other on the way.

When we, both friends and lovers,
do strive forward toward that shore,
I swear, my dear, that you
now delight me even more.

Poetry
by Crystal Gibbins

Lake of the Woods

Sometimes I visit the blue shores
where my father taught me how to fish.
I can hear the humming dark motor of his boat
gliding across the glassy water surface.
I imagine his ingenious grace
casting toward spirit-buoyant cattails,
steam rising from his thermos cup
as he stands in solitude at the edge of the cool wet stern
mirrored in the motion of waves.
On the islands around him, pines grow slow with secrets.
Standing like a stranger on the shore,
I look out across mute waters,
only to be spoken to by the mournful choir
of loons in the distance.

Poetry
by Linda Back McKay

Open Book

This lofty box of ink, blood and paper holds us
suspended in solidarity and solitude, this odd
juxtaposition of camaraderie and anonymity,

as readers fumble through the strange
houses of their night minds, as a stairway
goes nowhere but up and up is enough

within haunted transparent walls
to clatter dreams and odd snips of something
living. A sound times itself out, more solid

than mere earth under flesh feet, this magnetic
tapestry of echoes, this runaway picture show,
this wildfire of desire, this puddle of words.

Previously published in Linda Back McKay chapbook "The Cockeyed Precision of Time."

Fiction
by Todd Gulliver

Second Chance

Author's note: Inspired by the true story of my great-aunt Dorothy.

As the only doctor in Sawgrass County in 1912, Doc Johnson's seen his share of heartbreak: families torn asunder by disease, men's limbs torn from their bodies by farm equipment, women's hands mangled by those new machines for washing clothes, hunters shot, and children drowned. The sorrow seems endless. Each time he's patched up their bodies and their spirits as best he could. But this time it's different. This time he must decide what the heartbreak will be.

Ethyl and James Swenson handled the first stillbirth as well as any young bride and groom, the next three . . . not so well. Each pregnancy carried a bit longer than the previous, sucking more meat from her bones, withering her frame, and feeding her hope. He'd told them to avoid any more pregnancies; the next one might kill her. Abstinence was the price they'd have to pay to ensure a long life together. But here they were again. He couldn't blame them, but he wasn't sure she'd survive this time.

Ethyl and James had arrived at Doc's home at 3 a.m.

The borrowed farm truck sputters on like a beast refusing to die, announcing their arrival, as they struggle up the snowy walk in the bitter night air. Doc Johnson ushers them into the one time pantry, now examining room, nestled between his office and kitchen. James, unable to bear the suffering he blames himself for, slinks off to the front room to wrestle with his own burden. The hours pass slowly; Doc coaching and encouraging when Ethyl is conscious, then watching and praying when she slips into an exhausted stupor. Mrs. Johnson, accustomed to the occasional role as late night nurse, floats between them all, offering compassion, assistance and prayer.

During the dead calms while Ethyl is unconscious, Doc's

experienced eye appraises her physical and emotional reserves, balancing them against the struggles yet to come. At six months, it's by far the most developed she's delivered, but it's still smaller than it should be and as before there's little movement. Given her history and the size of the fetus, there's little hope in saving the child. Nursing and caring for a sickly infant in her condition might just kill her, if the delivery doesn't do it first. So that's it, he thinks, save the mother. And we might just have to take the child's life to do it. Hopefully it won't come to that. Hopefully the child will be stillborn again. It's looking that way now, but she's holding it in. She knows it's too early. Even with all this, she's still hoping to save this child.

In the end, Ethyl's heart is betrayed by her body, which follows its natural rhythms and pushes the fetus out, then collapses back into its stupor.

Now the hopes and fears of everyone in this house cascade onto Doc Johnson as he looks down at the tiny mewling infant quivering in his hands. This time he'll have to decide what the heartbreak will be. "It's not developed enough to survive," he thinks as he tenderly unwinds the umbilical cord from around the neck anyway, thumps her bottom, prays for the blue tinged skin to flush red, and waits for the howl of new life to fill the room and the rest of the house. The howl never comes and the blue fades only slowly. Then the worst happens; it's nothing Doc learned in school, just something he's picked up over the years. He knows when the life's spirit is present and when it's left. He's seen it leave many times, usually just as the body dies, but sometimes days before. And sometimes, he'd swear it was around for days after. But he's never discussed that with anyone; they'd think he wasn't "modern and enlightened." This infant girl's spirit had just left; he saw it, and now he's certain this body is nothing more than an empty shell. And yet the body still moves . . . weakly. Still breathes . . . occasionally. Glancing at Ethyl in her comatose state, he sets the infant in the slop pail held between his knees.

Gently, kindly, he cuts and ties the umbilical cord like the ribbon on a present he will never be able to deliver, then lays the used bandages and gauze over the infant. Handing the bucket to his horror-stricken wife, he murmurs, " . . . it's best for all . . . set this outside in the cold . . . but where the animals can't reach it . . . we'll retrieve it in a few hours time." As she stumbles toward the kitchen with a burden too heavy to bear, Doc calls out for James to come in from the front room.

Doc asks James to wake his wife as he musters his resolve. He has to do this now, while he's still busy, so it'll be less obvious that he can't look them in the eyes. "It's best you don't see the child . . . " he says gently, but is unable to continue.

On her way through the kitchen, Mrs. Johnson's footsteps slow to a shuffle, then stop as she stares horrified at the bandages, knowing an infant is buried below. Since Doc would never harm, let alone kill a human being, she knows that this infant has no chance of surviving. The bandages rustle one last time, then lie still. Feeling she must do something to acknowledge this life's passing, she begins a funeral prayer for the infant and a prayer of forgiveness for herself. Unaware that another soul is watching, she lifts the refuse to look on the face of this nearly dead infant. Hovering like a dove over Mrs. Johnson's shoulder, an unnamed soul peers into the blank eyes of the infant and decides, "This one will do just fine." As if pulling on a long lost coat, the spirit slips into the child's body, reviving head, chest, and then limbs.

Mrs. Johnson stares in disbelief as the blank eyes take on depth, the chest swells with air, and the arms and legs jostle the bloody bandages. Flushing red, the re-born infant announces her arrival with a hearty borning cry. Relief pours over Mrs. Johnson as she realizes her burden has been lifted. Setting the pail on the table, she lifts the infant from the cold steel tomb and wraps her in a dish towel. Hurrying back to the examining room, she's hit with Doc's anger and disbelief as she smiles, lays the infant on Ethyl's stomach and says, "Like Richard was saying, it's best you don't see the child until I've had a chance to clean her up. Congratulations. It's a girl!"

Epilogue

. . . she lived.
Dorothy Marie Swenson lived
to lead a life no other soul could have.
Not a glamorous life
nor a famous one
but quietly
gracefully
she moved through this world
leaving a trail of angel dust
and happiness
on every soul in her path.
She lived in the background
touching
and blessing
more lives than she
or they
ever knew.
Truly she lived.

Poetry

by John H. Thornberg

I Had Forgotten

Standing on the dock in light rain

I had forgotten how it rings,
the rain on mirrored pools,
how clear its hands applaud
Calliope in cadent voice
reciting Nature's eloquence.
I hear the silver coins of sound
tossed in her Parnassian spring,
and listen to the lilting tap
of Mother's fingers on her glass.

Poetry
by Louise Bottrell

Aftermath of Tuberculosis, 1948

My mother lies cold in the winter ground.
We sacrifice her rayon dresses on the pyre

of purification. The paisley designs curl
to temporal ashes, spiral across the hog lot,

snagging in weeds along the barbed wire
before crumbling to dust in the dark earth.

Creative Nonfiction
by Barbara Jacksha

Pigeons of Sante Fe

On Good Friday, we are penitents hauling a cart of groceries. Around us, clods of falling snow form a heavy, wet curtain; sloppy snowballs splat our heads. In the piñon trees bordering the parking lot, balls of fluff cling to the branches—pigeons huddled safe and dry while we, like oxen, coax stubborn wheels through unfurrowed snow.

"Excuse me," a woman says while we are thinking of the highway, hoping to pass through the foothills before the storm gets worse. "Excuse me," the woman says again. This time we turn. She's shivering beneath a black flannel shirt that hangs to her knees. Snow flocks her pueblo-baked skin and black, slicked-back hair. As she paddles water-soaked moccasins toward us, her red, raw fingers clutch a deformed globe of turquoise that dangles from a worn cord around her neck.

When the snow hits her face, she does not blink. She says she needs money for a hotel. She says all the shelters are full.

We smell alcohol on her breath.

We know about the scams, but it's Good Friday and the clods of snow are getting larger, denser, harsher now in a rising wind. We have eighteen dollars between us; we press it into her icy fingers, wishing it was more.

Her remaining teeth are brown stumps, and when she says "God Bless," there's the hiss of wind passing through a once-grand forest. Then she's gone, disappeared behind the snow curtain.

Will she take shelter? There's no way to know, so we load our groceries and climb into the car. We turn on the heater, brush snow from our arms, and warm ourselves with the hopeful feeling enjoyed by saints and fools.

Poetry

by Sharon Harris

Life-Worn

the old dog,
with several strokes behind her,
has lived more lives
than most cats.

she stands
at the corner
of her kennel
with aching joints.

her near-blind eyes
stare at the forest's edge.
she woofs quietly
at even intervals,
life-worn,

calling death,
asking the peaceful darkness
to come for her.

Poetry

by Charmaine Donovan

Last Night in Guadalajara

I will never forget
how we stood in the elevator
riding between the eighth floor
and the lobby until I knew
I must be crazy
yet could not help myself.
The words we dared not say
closed before us
like an elevator door shutting
before we were willing to leave.
The word *goodbye* stuck
to the threshold of our lips
because goodbye never enters a dream.
Still we had to go.

If I had met you in the park
with the peacocks, falcons,
the drums beating toward May 6th
instead of at the hotel pool,
perhaps we could have
made more of our meetings.
You were staying in this sunny place
where you were miserable,
something I could not begin to help
or understand.

For if misery could find you there,
even without a wife,
in a city where each flower opened
its fullest face to the sun,
in complete satisfaction
that could not go on forever,
then you were more hopeless
than a blade of grass
that has nowhere to grow.

Poetry
by Tarah L. Wolff
Too Late

She picked up after them,
napkins, paper plates,
silverware and such.

She pushed the chairs in,
fetched a stray from across the room,
on its side,
from a careless nudge.
No—a toss.
No—a throw.
Her throw.

She started a load of laundry,
turned on the dishwasher
and paused to listen to its woosh.

She thought of his retreat earlier,
during hour six of silence,
to the bedroom for a nap.

She gazed at the hallway, the doorway,
him on top of the covers.

Past 3 a.m.

She eased down into bed beside him
too late for any more fighting tonight.

Fiction

by Linda M. Johnson

Creating a Scene

The front door was open so the mail carrier stuck his head inside. “Hello, anybody home?" When Lainey came down the hallway wiping her hands on a dishtowel, he thrust a large envelope at her. "I'll need your signature," he muttered gruffly.

The envelope was official, complete with return receipt requested. Lainey felt the weight of it in her hands as she looked at the return address. Funny how one's life can be altered with the delivery of just one piece of mail. Postal carriers must be so proud, she surmised, changing peoples lives every day. She started chanting softly, "Neither rain nor storms nor sleet nor snow . . . "

A discreet cough. Lainey looked up. The mail carrier stood at the door. "Ma'am, could you sign the receipt." It was more statement than question. Pause. "Please?" He sounded like he was in a hurry. The bulging bag he carried indicated more work to be accomplished. More lives to change. "I have a pen right here," he added.

The light was shining on him from behind, his face in shadow. Lainey couldn't see his eyes. She wondered if he was smirking at her. Or if he knew what the envelope in her hand contained. A bubble of anger burst inside of her, but she didn't alter her expression.

"Yes, of course I’ll sign. But do you mind if I use my own pen?" she asked, the same time as she turned. "It's right here in the desk drawer," she continued, as she moved with measured steps towards the desk.

"Uh, okay, but this pen is fine," the mailman said, as he shifted the bag on his shoulder. "I really should get going, Ma'am."

Enough with this Ma'am business. Lainey opened up the drawer, grabbed what she needed. She quickly turned.

"I've got it right here," she said, as she pivoted on her heel. She looked at him again. Some letters dropped from his hands to the floor, unnoticed, as she assumed an exaggerated police stance. She aimed a pistol at his heart. The gun popped. A small white flag spurted out of the end. The mailman fainted, hit the floor with a thud while Lainey laughed wildly.

The phone rang, disrupting any thought.

"Hello," Kelli said. She was breathless after running to the phone.

"Kelli? Honey, are you okay?" John's voice was ripe with concern.

"I'm fine, just fine," Kelli said. She sighed deeply. "You caught me in the middle of . . . "

"Oh, great," John interrupted. "You weren't doing anything, then."

Kelli sizzled as John discounted her writing yet again. Just because she hadn't sold any stories yet didn't mean she wasn't a writer. That last critique on the scenes she'd written for the screenwriter had asked her to send in revisions on those scenes along with additional work to be looked at. John just didn't get it. Holding back a sarcastic retort took all of her concentration. "I was writing, John," she said, speaking slowly and succinctly. "You caught me in the middle of an important scene. Did you need something?"

John laughed softly, then seductively whispered, "I need you. Tonight. Will you be ready for me?" His pause was expectant. Hopeful. What a jerk, she thought. Ignores me, makes fun of my work, and expects me to roll over and . . .

"Hon? Are you still there?"

Kelli inwardly sighed while she tried to figure a way out of this. John was clearly expecting an amorous evening and, knowing him, he was at the end of an important case and had lots of energy to burn. God knows he had time to make up for. She thought quickly. She couldn't even remember the last time they'd made love. Doggone it and here she was on a roll with her writing. The words were flowing like the Mississippi. They'd started out as a trickle but had quickly gained momentum. Well, she had a couple of hours before he'd be home from work. She'd figure something out.

"Sure thing, Sweetheart. I can't wait until you get home." She tried to sound enthused. "See you later." Hanging up the phone, she sighed out loud this time. "What can I do to distract him?" was the question she pondered.

When John arrived home from work that night, Kelli was ready for him. Meeting him at the door, she didn't even speak. Instead, she reached for his briefcase and placed it near the closet. She reached out to loosen his tie. Holding the tie firmly in her hands, she pulled him down for a long, wet kiss. She put all the energy she had into the kiss. As she felt him respond, she broke contact. She winked at him, turned towards the kitchen, crooked her finger as in "follow me." Without looking behind, she hurried to the granite topped island, where she had two crystal glasses of wine already poured.

"Well, what have we got here?" John's voice was deep as he looked at her eagerly.

Handing him the wine she'd secretly spiked with a double dose of fast-acting sleep aid, Kelli didn't answer. Instead she said, "Drink up. To us." She raised her glass to meet his. They touched rims. She drank deeply, watching while he did the same. Putting her glass down, she said suggestively, "Let me top these off, then let's go somewhere more . . . comfortable." She licked her lips and nearly laughed as she watched his pupils dilate in pleasure. Men were so easily manipulated, she thought. "Finish up, Honey." She watched with gleeful anticipation as he downed the wine in a single gulp. She thoughtfully refilled his glass, then topped off her own. She took another drink before she motioned towards the bedroom.

John was yawning by the time he reached the edge of the bed. Reaching for his glass, Kelli made a show of placing it on the bedside table. Gently pushing John down on the bed, she was thankful for his sleepy eyes. Oh, I love real bedroom eyes, she thought. They were slowly closing as she leaned over and kissed his lips. He barely responded. "Good night, sweet dreams," she whispered, as his breathing became slow and regular.

The doctor had told her when she called to inquire about this over-the-counter medication that if alcohol was consumed with this particular sleep aid, it would act very quickly and was not recommended. It would do no harm, but the taker should be able to lie down within moments and should be able to devote "eight or more full hours to sleep," the Doctor said. Don't take it with a laxative, Kelli had added silently. Kelli thanked him for the information, pretending she'd been the one who had taken it after a drink so needed to know the consequences.

Kelli covered John with a soft chenille throw, then practically sprinted from the room. Once she was back in her office, she forgot all time as she continued to work on the screenplay she'd started.

Later, long after the mail carrier rebounded from his non-life-threatening wounds and secretly fell in love with the troubled, now-institutionalized Lainey, Kelli climbed into bed. John stirred in his sleep, but didn't awaken. Kelli snuggled under the blankets, then closed her eyes. What a great evening, she thought, as she drifted off into the deep sleep of the truly satisfied.

Poetry
by Doris Stengel

At the Clothesline

Lifting my arms
to hang a pillowcase,
my face turned upward
warms in daffodil sun.

On birch crown
cardinal whistles
for a mate
while the neighbor's cat
glides through grass
tail twitching.

I stoop, grasp corners
of a sheet, pin one end,
another pin midway
and one at hem end.
The sheet fills with April
pretending it's a sail.

The condominium complex
nearby forbids clotheslines
depriving residents
of this ancient ritual,
this bending and stretching
humble and praising,
usurping their right
to sleep in beds scented
with incense of resurrection.

Poetry

by Jerry Mevissen

Blue Mason Jar

Hot coffee streams down a knife in a Blue Mason jar.
"Keeps the jar from cracking," she says, then wraps
buttered bread in a dishtowel and packs it in a pail.

In the field, a man pitches hay onto a wagon.
Atop, a boy pulls the hay to the middle and stomps.
The horses stand, reins slung across their backs.
The man lifts his hat and wipes his brow of dust and sweat.
He sees her cross the field and motions to the boy.

She pours coffee, lukewarm, in stoneware mugs.
Sepia brown coffee, rich with cream.
The boy tastes sugar. That's how the man drinks his coffee.

The boy feeds flicks of clover to the horses while they talk.
The man sweeps his arm across the field of windrows.
He drinks his coffee and swings the cup in a wide arc.
She packs the cups and jar and returns.

Now, years later, when I taste sweet coffee,
I'm making hay on that Wisconsin farm.
Drinking Dad's coffee, sweet, the way he drank it,
poured from a Blue Mason jar.

Poetry – Honorable Mention
by Marlene Mattila Stoehr

Onion Tears

Evening. Nearly mealtime in our farm home.
My mother was carving remnants of Sunday's roast for hash.
One long ring on our wall telephone,
a call to Central on the party line.
I listened in. Everybody did.
It was this news I heard and had to tell:
"That was Mrs. Peterson. Ed just died."

Our neighbor, Ed Peterson, just died.
Settler farmers.
Our small farms were very near.
These parents shared the heartbreak
and the struggles of hard Depression years.
Pioneer Finnish families.
They neighbored. Sharing grownup secrets
children's ears were not to hear.

But Ed just died, and I,
not yet conscious of the unrelenting rules of death,
came to understand the strength of friendship that day.
I learned that some emotions
run too deep to be expressed in words.

"Ed just died."
My father heard me.
He sat a moment,
then without a word,
left his paper on the chair,
moved to the table,
and began to chop the onions for the hash.

Poetry
by Russell W. Jacobson

For Willie

May 1966. In a trifling breeze,
Willie sprinted the hundred
barefoot in nine-four.

We thought he would run his way
through college, letter, and graduate.
But no, in June he volunteered.

Tonight he is crossing the South
China Sea. He will taste its breath
as he steps from the plane. Within
days he will learn what makes
jungle monkeys scream at night.

Run your socks off, Willie, don't
let them catch you now.

Fiction

by Peggy Glynn

Love, Hate and the Highwayman

As usual, this morning the bus is a stage for Lenny Stine. His pesky hands grab my pony tail, always the teaser and showoff. Maybe the ignoramus will quit if I ignore him, a tactic that worked before. Cindy Stone is perched next to me, a nervous chipmunk holding her book like a handful of acorns, munching on every word.

Lenny grabs the absorbed Cindy's purse and finds her latest heartthrob note and begins to read it out loud. She lurches up and grabs at it but he keeps it just out of her range and continues his monologue in loud syrupy tones. She sinks back into her seat like a beaten mutt and shadows her face with her *Black Beauty* book. Cindy minds her own business. Cindy doesn't believe in toothbrushes or hair brushes at this point in her life and has told me, "My only friends are animals." At least she was reading about horses, something cool, as she won the Triple Crown of embarrassment. He had teased her before and I remember the other day watching her walk down her driveway gingerly stepping into the deep ruts made by the weekly visits from the milk truck. Her head lowered, her hair straggling down her back swept up occasionally by a gust of harsh wind. By the time her small frame reached the farmhouse door, tears had probably made deep ruts in her face.

I have no intention of letting anything of that sort happen to me. I'm prepared to defend myself with whatever it takes to smash Lenny.

Our bus is always cold in winter unless you get the seat with the heater where you get scorched. We were dubbed prairie dogs by the town kids and a few teachers because we were raised on the prairie fifteen miles northwest of town. We crisscross the frozen farmland and pick up the kids waiting at one bullet-hammered mailbox after another, vandalized by farm boys target practicing. With a forty-five minute bus ride, by the time we got to school, guaranteed, we are as antsy as if we had chowed on sugar for a week.

The bus squeals to a halt. I wait for Lenny and his buddies to get off. Minutes later, I'm grabbing the cold handle of the math room door.

The good thing about first hour is eighth grade Math. Not because I like it but the opposite. I hate it. I'm glad I get it over with at the beginning of the day because then the rest of the day doesn't seem so bad—usually.

Mr. Snodgrass, the eighth grade math teacher, is sort of like Lenny but planted in the body of a fifty-five year old, sagging at the neck, the midriff and probably at the knees, which I don't ever want to know as fact. You never know what kind of a mood he will be in. But for sure, *if* you're not naturally good in math you are fair game for ridicule. I *am the fairest of game.* I do the problems correctly during the week and then bomb the tests. I mean a C is a great thing to get on a math test for me. But usually it is a D and sometimes, like this time, the unmentionable.

I used to love the smell and feel of chalk until I met Mr. Snodgrass. He took all my love away. Today he starts the hour with, "People, I need you to be quiet," and rolls the chalk in his hands as he walks up and down the aisle lecturing about fractions. In the middle of the hour he hands back our tests on angles and my stomach immediately goes into the math lurch. I swallow down oatmeal gases that are finding their way back to my mouth.

"Miss Ryan," the chalk, an orb of white flying toward me, "you cheated," Mr. Snodgrass said. I had never seen his face so red. "There is no way you could get the answers right on your daily assignments and flunk the test. I am convinced you have been copying someone's daily assignments and so now will you please study the angle you find in the front left comer of the room," he says, with his forehead turning blotchy red, his left cheek twitching. "You will stand there for the remainder of the hour."

I toss my blond mop of hair so it will fall over half my face as I make the walk to the designated angle, head hanging. I pass Lenny the rat from the bus as he says, "Oh math whiz, where you going?" Then a loud slap echoes the room as Snodgrass' ruler hits Lenny's desk. "Leonard Stine, that will be enough," he says. I reach the comer and stand limp as a wounded bird.

Fixed in misery, I try to get my mind off the hopeless thought that without any effort at all, Lenny has won another round. I melt at the thought that the kids in the room are watching my backside. Why didn't I wear my cowboy boots instead of these tacky dime store sneakers? Then I remembered my boots were full of manure because I had to get my horse back in the barn before school. I didn't have time to clean them. At least I have on my favorite jeans. We were called prairie dogs and I was beginning to feel like one.

I want my mind out of this cage. I want to scream but I can't. Then, like a robin in spring, the poem "The Highwayman" comes back to me. If I memorize it, I get twenty extra points in English class. I whisper the words:

"The wind was a torrent of darkness among the gusty trees,
The moon was a ghostly galleon tossed upon cloudy seas,
The road was a ribbon of moonlight over the purple moor,
And the highwayman came riding—
Riding—riding—
The highwayman came riding, up to the old inn-door."

I can hear the hoofs beating the dusty road. Bess is bound tightly with a musket at her breast. I smell the musty inn and its stifling mugginess. The redcoat soldiers use her love as a weapon that warns them.

"They said no word to the landlord; they drank his ale instead,
But they gagged his daughter, and bound her to the foot of her narrow bed.
Two of them knelt at her casement, with muskets by their side;
There was Death at every window,
And hell at one dark window,
For Bess could see, through her casement, the road that he would ride."

I wondered at the love Bess had for the Highwayman. How could there be such love to die for when she had so much to live for? Math never posed such questions. It always added up; at least it was supposed to. Boring, boring, boring.

I wandered through the rest of the poem like a lost puppy eating every morsel of passion it brought and feeling for Bess, my soul mate.

My mind is far, far away from my corner of the math room, when a shot rings out. Was it the musket sending its slug into the breast of Bess?

"You're excused, Miss Ryan."

"Ahh, what?"

I spin around. It's Snodgrass rolling his chalk with his stubby fingers, the second hour bell yet blasting. I am free. I grab my books and race out the door, avoiding his condescending gaze.

My eyes lock with Lenny Stine's as I pass through the door. His slanted sneer is branded on the dark side of my heart forever.

Poetry
by Scott Stewart

rhapsody in gray
(a cappella)

silly child quit playing
you're getting in the way
jabber close that screen door
it's too hot today
sinatra on the player
phrasing that last word
a covered porch with day old bread
for the hungry birds

maybe you can see it
maybe you cannot
maybe it doesn't matter
'less you passed through with that lot

jabber quit that skittin'
don't slack me no hack
don't spendin' all that money
or I'll never let'cha back
sybil writes her letters
waiting for true love
doesn't ever look up
knows not what's above

rain pours out its laughter
thunder rolls the ears
lightning fractures clouds
assaulted by the years

silly child quit toying
the cat has caught the mouse
black and white snapshots
come to life in this old house
age has painted pictures
of time on these sideboards
and the paint has chipped and faded
like a misplaced
                    childhood chord

Creative Nonfiction
by Beth Bradley Walter

Out of the Mouths of Babes

Don't trust anyone over thirty. It was a popular mantra of teenagers during the 60s. And yes, I'm old enough to remember that. This is probably why I am too old to use the popular slang of today's youth, according to my 17-year-old son.

It was an innocent mistake. I was simply watching television and made a casual reference to a certain 40-something guy as "hot." It so happens I was busted. "Mom," my son Andy said, sounding more than a little disgusted, "no one over thirty is hot—maybe attractive, but not hot." I burst out laughing. Not a little chuckle, but an enormous, endorphin-releasing belly laugh. I was tempted to retrieve his baby book from the cedar chest and make one final entry under "cute" things he said as a child.

As the day progressed, I continued to muse about the plight of us poor middle-aged folks and our lack of, well, hotness. If we can't be hot, then we must not be able to go on "hot dates" anymore. We are doomed to a purgatory of "pleasant evenings." And, not to get too personal, but we can probably forget about steamy sex, if hot dates are out of the question. Maybe if we eat enough fiber, exercise and get plenty of sleep, we can still count on "comforting affection" to sustain us in our golden years.

Gee, now I can hardly wait to get up in the morning and toss down a Geritol with wild abandon, slide on my sensible shoes and seize the day. Maybe I'll find an "attractive" man at the grocery store and we can shamelessly discuss the ripeness of melons with only a hint of a blush on our cheeks. Who says I still can't have a little fun?

Poetry
by Connie Claire Szarka

Brother Willie

Brother Willie, only three, rode off one day
and never came back.
That look in his *eyes*—
I've seen in our prairie men.
Willie got it
right there in front of McAbe's Five and Dime
when Mother said, "You's a good boy, Willie,"
and set him astride the nickel pony machine,
plugging it with a coin
from her egg money.

Will gripped the reins in tight fists
and never let go.
Galloping out of town,
across the fields
toward dusky mountains
and painted canyons,
he left our mother behind,
her strong hands keeping him balanced in the saddle.

Creative Nonfiction
by Andrew Scott Browers

Of Mike and Men

The fact that Mike Lukens was not beaten to a bleeding mush every day of his life is proof that there is a God whose love surpasseth understanding. A runty, red-haired aspiring medical research scientist seems the perfect incarnation of nature's kick-me sign. Yet Mike Lukens lived, mostly unscathed, to fight another day again and again. But that is not the largest of his miracles.

Mutual scorn and admiration brought us together. We each were somehow drawn to the other's mind, too eager for its own fifth grade good, like moths to the zapper. Perhaps we might have locked horns a time or two to defend or claim the uncoveted status of omega male, but we knew it would end in stalemate. Unable to shake our strange fascination, it was only inevitable that we would become pals. Of course, we were hardly the boy geniuses we thought ourselves, in secret, to be. Our combined intellect was less impressive than our combined collections of comic books.

"If Jor-el knew Krypton was doomed, why didn't he take his whole family to Earth?"

There would come a long, pregnant pause, interrupted at last by a weighty sigh.

"You don't get it, Andy," Mike would say with feigned patience and leave it at that. He was right. But I didn't get a lot of things.

Summers became synonymous with that house on Selmser Avenue. His insomniac mom would be sprawled on the couch well into the afternoon begging for sleep while her husband listened to *Who* tunes and drank nothing but diet Mountain Dew from morn 'til night. The Lukens' larder was bare more often than not—an inconvenience of economics misunderstood by growing boys—and the Herculean search for edible things seemed unending. We were occasionally allowed to split a can of the sacred nectar between us, but ambrosia was hard to come by.

Upon our mighty ten speeds, the summers were ours for the taking. Visits to *Rusty's*, the local comic book shop, to browse boxes of *Superman* and the *X-Men* were a sacred routine—a pilgrimage in search of holy tomes illustrated in primary colors. From there, we might head to the playground to unwrap and swap cards or exchange discoveries of the geekiest nature. Thick as thieves, you might say, we were with our shared love of those things. Another of our shared loves was a girl named Jackie, a blonde vision of eyes like the sky and dimples. I had seduced her into playing with us at recess, but that wasn't quite satisfying enough. I wanted to be able to walk beside her in the hallway and sit by her during group work and snack breaks. She was miles out of my league, I always told myself, but she has since confessed to me that I was her first crush. To think—all those misspent breaks eating my Cheez-Its in solitude.

To add to the image of coolness you undoubtedly have constructed of me and my young cohort, it should be known that we were in 4-H. For me, the club was the heirloom of my bloodline, passed through purple-ribbon-winning forebears. Mike had no excuse, other than I was in it and that made it awesome.

We graduated, by varying degrees, from the religion of superheroes and Saturday mornings to the worship of music and grown-up things. It was a slow process, spanning the early part of our teenage years. Those are the times I think of most fondly when the pleasant specter of adolescence comes to haunt me. That was the era of one of the few—and yes, I have known a small handful—miracles I have seen.

It seems that it never should have happened at all, one of those fleeting moments of idiotic pith ignored by most. But it was a statement too bold to be ignored.

"You could not," I said, ever the doubter even among my friends. "Nobody could."

Mike Lukens adjusted his glasses by scrunching his nose. "Wanna bet?"

I laughed, because, well, it was laughable. "Yeah, Mike. I bet you can't."

We shook on it. What followed has come to be a crux in my

private mythology.

Some time passed, weeks or months, until August rolled around, hot and swollen—State Fair season. Because we were awesome and in 4-H, the State Fair had become a familiar place over the years—the sum of all projects, exhibits, and animals. Since Mike Lukens and I had no animals to show for ribbons, we relied on other ways to the Fair, particularly in the ironically named event called Share-the-Fun, for which our club won first place in the skit category. Share-the-Fun had brought us here to test the limits of mortal endurance. Share-the-Fun, so innocent and unassuming, could have been blamed for the most gruesome death ever achieved. Share-the-Fun might have been Mike Lukens' one-way ticket to everlasting peace. But that love beyond human reason must have intervened and sent Share-the-Fun back to the dark abyss from whence it came, empty-handed and without supper. In the meantime, Mike Lukens was about to sup with destiny, and other horrors.

We stood before the *Teeny Weeny Donut* hut, eyeing both the prize and the obstacle. "Mike," I said. "You don't have to do this." I didn't want this tugging at my conscience for all my years to come. I had done enough stupid things to keep my guilt complex going. "I believe you, okay?" But I didn't and he saw through me with X-ray eyes.

Mike Lukens approached the counter, pulled from his pocket a greasy wad of bills and calmly ordered seven bags of *Teeny Weeny Donuts*.

The lady taking orders snapped her gum as her eyes grew wide in terror and awe. I will never forget the phrase she uttered, which may not have even been English. "*Holyshitisthatallforyoooou?*" She stopped chewing.

Mike shifted. "No," he said. "It's for my family." But she had guessed it right, and he returned with seven bundles of steaming fried doughnuts and about four gallons of Mountain Dew—and not of the *diet* variety. Holy shit it was all for him. I would estimate that on his person, Mike Lukens carried roughly sixteen thousand calories at that moment, all of which were heading in one direction: the pit of his stomach. And so it began.

Bag one went down with ease. He even chewed with flare to show how little such a feat would faze him. Bag two followed suit, though he did require a swig of pop here and there to wash bits of dead *Teeny Weeny Donuts* down the hatch. Three wasn't bad. At four, he had to take breaks between bites. At five, beads of sweat appeared on his brow and his breathing became labored. At bag number six, I thought he might lose consciousness. Each eye-rolling burp threatened to bring with it the compacted remains of his dangerous snack. More and more he relied on his Mountain Dew until he had sucked it dry. Bag seven sat on his lap among the empty and disheveled wrappers, still warm with grease and clumps of sugar.

"Come on Mike, one more." Screw the bet. I wanted to see him triumphant, though terms of victory and loss were never even established. This was for glory and for death. "One. More."

His body defeated and his mouth unable to produce its own saliva, his only weapon was his will. Melting the ice in his cup, Mike Lukens polished off the last bag with a muffled groan and clutched his gut, which had visibly expanded against his Green Day T-shirt and threatened to split down its center. He looked to the carnage that lay before him and he looked to me for assurance that he had done it. I beamed back at him, and I thought he was about to smile, but the sickly thing that spread across his lips was anything but. "I have to take a world-class crap," was all he said.

He had done it. He had eaten seven bags of *Teeny Weeny Donuts* in one sitting. I was in the presence of a titan, a god among doughnut eaters, and I could call him my friend. Sure, he could be kind of a wiener sometimes, but what hero doesn't have his tragic flaws? A hero he was and a hero he might remain, but I can't be sure. His legend has outlived our friendship, but I suppose that is somehow fitting of such a fellow—one more god in my personal little pantheon.

Long live Mike Lukens. That is what I say.

Poetry
by Tarah L. Wolff

Barbed Wire

A ten year old girl running full-tilt
through the woods.
It reached up, hidden in knee high grass,
threw her to the ground
ripped her jeans,
and took her breath away.

A fifteen year old girl walking along
property lines.
Still guarded by dilapidated barbed wire.
Came upon a union of steel and northern pine.
Tree grown around metal,
metal grown into tree.
A big change to accommodate
a life partner.

An eighteen year old girl flying south
to meet hubby's family.
Barbed wire hung on the wall down there,
in every shape and size, a wicked art piece,
proud as punch.
In-laws laid booby traps in knee high grass,
throwing the Yankee to the ground
dashing hopes, dreams
and took her breath away.

A twenty year old girl all wrapped up
in him.
In southern barbed wire.
She learns that even northern pines
can grow to accommodate
a life partner.

Poetry

by Susan Niemela Vollmer

Woodsmoke

If I were to name a new cologne
I'd call it woodsmoke

Dusky undertones
Enhanced by a light note of pine

A breath of applewood, hint of moss
Over a woody birch base

The scent would start off intensely
Then slowly dissipate

Leaving behind
Only a wisp of shared laughter

Fiction

by Sandra Edlund

The Necklace

It was right before I left when I saw it there in a glass case beside the cash register. I had just finished my shopping, buying two purses instead of one and spending a lot more than I intended. Trying to make a quick exit out the door, I almost missed it. There, surrounded by the castoffs of rich women, Prada, Coach and Armani, was a beautiful stone necklace draped around a headless mannequin. And before I could speak, a shop clerk was already removing it from the glass case saying, "Go ahead, try it on. See how it looks on you.

"It just came in today," the clerk said as he draped it around my neck. The stones were turquoise and rose quartz interspersed with shiny purple and navy glass beads. I admired my reflection in the glass as I played with the beads, twisting the stones to make a choker and then letting them hang between my breasts. "How could anyone sell such a beautiful necklace?" I asked.

"The woman who owned the necklace died recently," the clerk was saying. "Her son brought her old clothes and jewelry in just this morning. It looks beautiful on you," he said but his flattery was wasted. I was already hooked.

"I'll take it," I said. The shop clerk put it in a bag and I took the dead woman's necklace home.

At home, I hid my expensive bags in my sweater drawer and admired my last guilty purchase, the necklace. I rubbed the smooth stones between my fingers like rosary beads and tried to imagine the life of the previous owner, the woman with the turquoise necklace.

She was obviously a woman of taste and sophistication. I decided to call her Genevieve, a name befitting a woman of style. I could see Genevieve dancing under a stone arch in Barcelona, necklace swirling above her multicolored peasant skirt rising and falling to her knees as she danced the Flamenco. I could see her laughing as she danced with her lover as the molten sun burned her bare back. She probably danced barefoot on the beach, her feet studded with soft grainy sand.

Genevieve, you must have been a woman who liked the sea and untamed places like forests and beaches. A woman of the earth, solid and unbreakable like the turquoise stones; you were not an ethereal being gilded in gold or silver.

I can see you cradling your baby son as he tries to grab the necklace with small hands sticky sweet with baby gurgle.

And I can see your husband gently lift wispy tendrils of your hair as he hooks the stones around your neck. You smile and tilt your head back as he curls his arms around your waist and your face glows like a rosy jewel.

And in the end, when you could dance no more, when your legs grew stiff and your fingers bent and gnarly, you stopped wearing the necklace. Like a pressed flower you were until you crumbled back to the earth.

All that is left are your memories embedded in jewels. Genevieve, I feel your spirit as I caress these stones, your necklace, and I think about what you passed on to me. I hold not just a necklace, a mere string of beads, but a remnant of your life, your legacy.

Poetry
by Anne Musial

She Grows, She Sleeps

The line appeared quickly,
Faster than light,
I sit in shock, in fear, delight.

A new life is growing, a new soul is here.
Inside my own, it becomes so clear.
Immediately a mother, I plan, I wait,
For an outcome I could never anticipate.

She grows, she moves, she plays, she sleeps
She's wanted, she's named, adored so deep.

Christmas morn, my heart is anxious,
I am not even sure why.
She's still, she's quiet, she's heavy.
In the shower, I beg, I cry.

We drive in silence, the tears fall fast.
I already know deep down.
I reassure others that all is well,
Somewhere some strength is found.

The nurses work fast, they panic,
Chaos, this cannot happen today,
They won't look at us, only each other,
They are not allowed to say.

The doctor appears, dressed up
For Christmas in her red and green.
I am sorry, she says, no movement,
No heartbeat can be seen.

Then the fog, the blurry dream,
Of friends and family near,
Am I awake? Am I asleep?
No pain, no feeling, just fear.

They wake me softly; it's time.
"Just do the best you can."
Now she's leaving my body, resistant.
I'm holding someone's hand.

I hold her. I kiss her, her mouth slightly open,
As if to speak, to cry.
She's just so perfect, so loved, adored.
Now we must say good-bye.

Sweet girl, wherever you are
Your short life in my heart to keep.
Inside my mind, a better place for all time,
You grow, you play, you move, you sleep.

Poetry
by Jere Truer

The Robin

Some days are like this:
Scrambled eggs on a plate on the table,
Half eaten; a bagel; coffee getting cold.
I am distracted by the open-beaked
Confused terror of the robin outside
My window, perched on the fence for one
Restive moment before pingponging
Between my pane and the one next door.

Today is a beautiful day mid-June:
The fifteenth one in a row of this war
Of conflicting reflections. What does he
See each time he launches at the glass?
A way out which betrays him? A rival
Whom he must defeat in this nesting
Season? An enemy who is not there?
A part of himself forever cut off?

He appears played out, defeated but not
Giving up, willing to take a half-
Hearted stab once again as I see
Him hover at the window, punch drunk
Prize fighter in the fifteenth round
Unaware that the fight has been fixed.
I can only hope he finds his way home.
I'd give him the sky if I could.

Poetry
by Angela L. Beaumont

Snow Paintings

It sugars through the trees
Some clinging to shaggy pines
Making patterns I cannot emulate
On this unblemished paper.

I am in a domed, glass ornament
Shaken up
Snowflakes swirl
Hypnotizing me.

They kiss the ground
Whisper soft
Like the wing of a butterfly
On my arm.

The canvas is complete
Marshmallow cities
Cast indigo shadows
Under silvery light

Earth hunkers in for the night.

Fiction

by Kathryn Kirmis Medellin

The Lilac Bush

She peered through the large glass window waiting for me. My grandmother, Elizabeth Maria Wirtz. Wisps of gray hair escaped from under her babushka. Her cane in her right hand, she struggled to unbend her stooped frame. She wanted to impress me that she was not the frail person her body presented. I smiled as I got out of the car and walked to the door.

I looked forward to our journey. A journey to the country. No need to tell me where she wanted to go. We always went to the same place, had the same conversations, and sat on the steps of the old farmhouse. Sitting on those steps always provoked memories from my grandmother.

"Oh, Leeza, how nice of you to come. I am ready. Just point the way to the car." I felt special with my grandmother. She had comforted me as a child, and listened to my thoughts and dreams as I grew older. Elizabeth was my given name, named after my grandmother, but people called me Liz. Only my grandmother called me Leeza.

"You are a Leeza to me. Did you know your grandfather called me Leeza? It was his very special name for me. You remind me of myself when I was young."

She walked to the car as gingerly as she could, refusing to take my arm. "Don't let me shuffle," she told me several years ago. "I just don't want to shuffle!"

As we drove away, she waved to Mike, one of the elderly gentlemen who lived in the rest home.

"Someone you know?" I asked with a mischievous grin.

"Yes, but not in a serious way. I'm through with heartthrobs. They don't interest me in that way anymore."

I glanced at her face and saw the "you don't know what I am really thinking" look. I loved my grandmother.

Leaving the paved highway, we drove down the old country road graveled now but once a dirt track leading to the farmhouse.

"Do you see those wooden fence posts? I helped your grandfather put those in the ground. They had to be exactly straight.

No leaning posts for him."

I had heard the story before, and the one about the old windmill still standing but relieved of its labors long ago. No blades to turn in the wind, no mechanism to pull the water from the ground, no cattle to drink from the tank now rotted and long gone. It stood there, a reminder that it too had grown old, but not useless. It made my grandmother feel good just looking at it. How could something be useless if it made someone feel good?

We sat on the shaded steps of the back door. Wooden steps with a hundred spikes pounded into them. I knew there were one hundred because I had counted them a hundred times.

"You know why those nails are in the steps?" she asked me. Yes, I knew but she would tell the story again.

"When the boys got into trouble, I gave them twenty nails and a hammer. It took them awhile to pound them into the steps. They soon got rid of their naughty energy!" She was far ahead of her time—good therapy for her active sons.

It was comfortable sitting there, sometimes listening to my grandmother, sometimes listening to the warm July breeze rushing through the uncut dry grasses, sometimes enveloped in our own thoughts.

We didn't walk the farm as we usually did, not even to the lilac bushes where she would pick a leafy branch to take with her and put in her farm vase. The vase my grandfather had given her the first year they were married. I often thought the lilac bushes were very special to my grandmother, something she had never shared. I was curious, but I didn't want to intrude.

The afternoon slipped by, and after a lengthy silence my grandmother said, "Leeza, before we go, would you pick a branch from the lilac bush, the bush nearest the windmill?"

We walked to the car; my grandmother turned to look at the house, the windmill standing like a skeleton in the late afternoon sun, the lilac bushes. I opened the car door; she put her hand on my arm to steady herself, and as she got in, smiled at me and said, "One leg at a time." How often had I heard her say, "One leg at a time!"

"Yes, Leeza, that was a nice visit, but it's time to go now." She took off her babushka, placed it in her lap, folded her hands, and fell silent. I knew she would soon nod off.

As we drove along, I glanced at my grandmother, noticing

her hands, translucent and smooth, her sleeping face, the gray and black babushka, the hem long gone, the threads pulled loose, and the green lilac branch lying in her lap.

Grandmother still slept as I pulled into the parking lot and turned the key to shut off the engine. I got out and walked to her side of the car, opened the door to help her get out "one leg at a time."

"We're home," I said to my grandmother. There was no answer. I looked at her still figure and then I recalled that just before we left the farm she had wistfully said, "It's time to go."

Four years have passed since that day. I drive alone to the old farm place, sit on the steps, count the nails, listen to the wind. Before I leave, I walk to the lilac bush, the one by the windmill, pick a leafy branch to put in the farm vase, and pause a minute to wonder what was so special about that lilac bush.

Poetry
by Marianne McNamara
Isabella in the Snow

I sleep and snow falls . . .

settles thickly on windowsills,
drifts deeply over graveyard crosses and headstones,
covers familiar streets with zigzags of velvety chenille.
The worn-out neighborhood where I've lived
for too many years transforms into alabaster splendor.

The alarm goes off and he brushes
tangled hair from my cheek,
whispers against my ear that it's snowing.
I peek out expecting a few patches
but everything is buried under layers of white.

I raise the old spring roller shade,
force open my frozen window to breathe icy air,
lean my forehead against cool smooth glass
watch my breath spread in a foggy cloud.
I think maybe we'll be snowed in together all day.

Then I see them in the backyard snow,
a chain of footprints
linking enormous block letters
carved with a broom handle,
letters that make my heart smile . . .

ISABELLA I LOVE YOU

Poetry

by Judy Sladek

The Chosen

Cut from some age-old rock,
the small north shore stones
can hardly believe the long
journey.

Water and wind have led them,
finally, to the center
of my soft warm palm,
to be rubbed and rubbed and rubbed,

because if they weren't here
they would be somewhere else,
the rhythmic dance of wind and water
grinding them to dust.

Poetry

by Marion C. Holtey

Denali

On this September morning
I stand silent, shivering
beneath mighty mountains

sprinkled with early snow
quaking with golden aspen
below a turquoise sky.

Miles away, draped in grey clouds,
North America's tallest peak,
"The Great One" is visible.

Asians discovered sacred Denali
ages ago when they trekked across
the Bering Strait to Alaska.

Today I listen to a descendant
standing on a glacial boulder
drumming ancient stories.

With eyes closed, he chants
respect for the earth, for all people
and honor for the Great Spirit.

The fur of his parka frames
his weathered face as he beats
the spirit of his Athabascan people.

Silently my pulse echoes
the beat of his well-worn drum.

Fiction – Honorable Mention
by Anne M. Dunn

Dirty Indians

George One Road had been drinking for several days when he tumbled into a ditch full of cold water and fell on his face. Suddenly he was sober enough to acknowledge the empty ache in his belly and realize that he hadn't eaten since the day before yesterday. Physically tormented by such prolonged hunger, he turned his reluctant feet toward home.

Daylight was pressing against the windows when Minnie put aside her embroidery, cupped her hand over the chimney of the kerosene lamp, and blew it out. Almost simultaneously, she heard her husband fumbling at the door of their small house. She stepped to the middle of the room but ignored his clumsy efforts to get inside. When he finally flung the door open and stumbled into the sparse but cozy front room, she gave him a long, icy stare and turned her back on his painful remorse.

Once inside, George didn't feel so hungry anymore and he knew he couldn't ask Minnie for food now. He looked around the room and saw five-year-old Tillie asleep in the big chair. He saw Minnie's contempt, too. But he put a shoulder against her coldness and pushed his way back into their lives. He forced his heavy feet to climb the narrow stairway to their attic bedroom. His face was already twisted into a grimace of self-hatred when he fell across the old chenille spread that covered the brass bed.

Tillie was awake now. Quietly she slipped from the chair and crept up the worn wooden steps behind her father. She covered him with her tattered doll blanket and curled up beside him. George smiled and turned to face her. Then he wrapped his arms around her warmth, kissed her pretty nose, and fell into a peaceful sleep.

When Minnie heard her husband begin to snore, she went up the stairs, too. As she gazed down on her dear ones, Tillie looked up at her and smiled.

Minnie spread a large warm quilt over her husband and child. Then with the light touch acquired over long years of experience, she picked his pockets as Tillie watched. She found a brass whistle, a small jack knife, a bottle opener, a few crumpled bills and a handful of coins. She put the coins in her pocket, rolled the paper money into a tight bundle, and removed a large shiny knob from the bed. Then she tucked the money inside, replaced the knob and went down the stairs. Tillie slipped out of her father's arms and followed her mother to the kitchen.

The pantry was located under the attic stairs and when Minnie opened the pantry door, Tillie crept back into its dark depths. Moments later she emerged with a red and white baking powder can. Without rising to her feet, Tillie removed the lid and her mother stooped down to place the coins inside. Then she replaced the cap and returned the can to its hiding place.

Later, Minnie busied herself at the woodstove and soon the aroma of bacon and coffee wafted itself invitingly over the sleeping man. Slowly his eyes opened. He stretched, yawned and finger-combed his tousled black hair.

He touched the quilt and smiled toward the rafters, grateful for his wife's consideration of his comfort. For a single moment, he was happy. But his happiness turned to guilty shame as he recalled his binge drunk. He didn't know how he could face his family again. Nevertheless, he got up and went down the stairs.

Minnie had filled the chipped enamel basin with warm water and hung a clean towel on a nail over the washstand. His clean clothes were folded neatly on a kitchen chair. Like an obedient child, he stripped, bathed, and dressed without resistance.

When he was fit to sit, Minnie put a dish heaped with food at the head of the table and poured two cups of strong coffee. As George sat down to eat, Minnie picked up her cup and went to sit near the front window where Tillie sat on the floor quietly playing with her rag doll and a small tattered blanket.

Minnie didn't speak to her husband all that day. There was nothing she could say. There was nothing he could say . . . it had all been said before. Their silence fell around the child like ash from a forgotten fire.

But the next morning Minnie gave him some money and

he took Tillie to the general store in the white man's village. Hand in hand they walked along. Together they watched bluebirds swim through a bright sky and golden butterflies dance with windblown flowers.

At the store Tillie carefully selected a few pieces of penny candy and a Bit-O-Honey. She got a Butterfinger for Mama and George purchased a bag of Bull Durham cigarette tobacco. When he asked for a book of matches, the skinny proprietor scowled and handed them to him. But as George reached for them with trembling fingers, the proprietor laughed mirthlessly and let them fall on the counter between them.

George pulled himself into a military posture, picked up the matches and met the other man's staring blue eyes. "Thank you, kind sir," he said with exaggerated tones of grateful esteem. Then he brushed his thick hair back from his face in a manner that made the white man acutely aware of his own bald head.

Then George turned to leave. He and Tillie had already reached the door when the proprietor muttered a string of epithets that ended with "those dirty Indians."

Later they walked to the small public park and George pushed Tillie on the swing. The rusty scream of the old chain irritated the man but it thrilled the child. Higher and higher she flew until she felt the clouds touch her upturned face. Then she closed her eyes and kissed the bottom of the sky.

When a group of loud, blond children arrived, George took Tillie from the swing and they quickly left the park. But not before she'd heard one of the boys say, "Those dirty Indians think they own our park!"

That's when George picked Tillie up, swung her over his head and set her on his shoulders. She felt very tall as she bobbed along, and very proud of her strong father.

Later they stopped to watch a mallard hen and nine fluffy ducklings feed in the water-filled ditch near the dusty road. Tillie tried to coax them to her with a piece of candy.

George laughed. "Ducks don't eat candy. Next time we'll bring some bread."

Tillie could already hear her mother. "What! I wear myself out around here trying to keep us fed and you want to feed my good bread to a duck."

Just then a car came along. Someone leaned from the window and shouted, "Get out of the road, you dirty Indians."

George took Tillie's small hand and pulled her along until the car was out of sight. Then he waited patiently as she stopped to pick up a few pretty stones for Mama. She held them up for him to see but he was far away now . . . lost in thoughts.

Minnie called him Moody when he pulled himself into his shell. Tillie knew they would linger here and there along the way for hours. She knew they would not reach home until the stars came out. She knew he would not speak and she was silent, too.

At last they reached home and when Minnie saw the helpless anger smoldering in her husband's troubled eyes, she prayed for one more sober day. Just one.

Then she prepared a meatless supper and they made happy chatter around their small table. Later she surprised her family with cookies and lemonade, an extravagance purchased with her secret coins.

That night Minnie washed Tillie's face, neck, and ears. Tillie washed her own hands and feet. Then she put on her faded pink pajamas and George carried his sweet smelling baby up the stairs to her cot under the east window. He was in a good mood now so he told her a story about a little girl and a blue butterfly. Then he tucked the blanket carefully around her.

When he leaned down to kiss her, Tillie wrapped her small arms around his neck and pulled his ear to her mouth. "You're my big dirty daddy," she whispered, "and I'm your little dirty girl."

There was a war inside of George that night. He didn't like to think about how it was going to end, so he went out and found his brother, Richard.

Three days later, he came home tired, hungry, and unwashed.

Minnie waited as he fumbled at the door and wept as he disappeared up the attic steps.

Then Tillie crept up the stairs to cover him with her small blanket.

Poetry
by Larry Schug

On That Rainy Sunday

(for Roger Young)

I didn't know,
though you might have,
that you'd be gone by Monday;
a good soul
driving a broken-down truck
on a ten mile downhill run
with nine miles worth of brakes.
You couldn't get out of bed,
your body ravished by that god damn cancer,
yet when I entered your room
a light ignited in your eyes,
you hugged me with bony arms
like all your wood-cutter's strength
had returned, summoned by sheer willpower.
As I pressed my face into your neck,
you must've felt my tears, warm on your skin;
tears of joy as much as of grief,
both of us knowing that all the years
had come down to this one moment
and that this moment would have to last
forever.

Poetry
by Sandra Jane Larson
Cross Country Skiing

Burnished with a hard blue wax, my skis
slip into these woods—the jack pine,

the juniper, the spruce. I'm learning
to glide, to relax, to pole,

not push, in the two-lined tracks.
Deeper into the woods, cold

whispers between purple pine shadows;
a cardinal in the throat of winter

holds the world stark white
against himself and sings.

Needles of evergreen boughs stand
in pristine attention.

The air like a mint
is formal.

The contours of winter,
nearer the deeper I go; and

deeper still,
the stillness I'm skiing through.

Poetry

by Debbie Pea

January in Minnesota

Tires groan on snowy driveways.
Boots crunch into squeaky snow.
All the people look like bundles
when it's ten or twenty below.

Winter's icy tendrils twine
around my body, claiming me.
I surrender to the shivering—
only warmth will set me free.

I thought it was too cold to snow
and yet the air persists and makes
snow from moisture hardly present.
Dry, itchy skin makes different flakes.

Wind whips up a gypsy dance
of snowflakes not yet matted down
while evergreens stand on the sidelines
wearing winter like a gown.

Sun so bright and ground so white.
The sky—uninterrupted blue.
The deep red cardinals stay all winter,
knowing they enhance the view.

Winter harshness and its beauty
wrestle in my thoughts today
as I long for warmth of summer
and it seems so far away.

I fear and curse the blizzards,
then with wonder I admire
the Minnesota winter's
power to torment or inspire.

The greatest power of winter is
the hope and joy that it can bring
as it takes a bow and exits,
after introducing spring.

Creative Nonfiction
by Jerry Mevissen

Romance of the Rails

At one o'clock on a March morning, the Staples Railroad Depot is deserted, dark, and foreboding. The doors are open, however, and the waiting room is warm. The Empire Builder left Chicago 12 hours earlier and is due at 1:42 A.M. There is no ticket agent at the depot, no baggage check, no Starbucks kiosk. Only me. Will the train arrive on time? Will it stop? Where will I board? It's one o'clock in the morning, and Staples streets have rolled up for the night.

A pickup truck arrives carrying a passenger. Then a car, and two more passengers. Yes, I am told, the train will be on time, it will stop, and we will board where we're standing. We will carry our own luggage aboard. A conductor will detrain and assign us to cars, based on our destination.

At 1:46, the Amtrak Empire Builder sounds its whistle and glides into Staples. Engine, sleeper, dining car, coach cars, another sleeper. The cars are sleek, stainless steel, double decked. The train slows to a halt, and a door opens from inside. Two conductors dismount, one carrying a yellow steel step which he sets before the door. One conductor boards passengers for end-of-the-route destinations—Portland and Seattle. The second conductor radios to the engineer to advance three car lengths. He examines my ticket. "Get on board," he says. We board the seventh of an eight car train.

I carry skis over my shoulder and a soft suitcase in each hand. No baggage check, no security inspection, no smiley stewardess to welcome me aboard. I stow the skis in an overhead compartment of a lower car and walk up a narrow, winding stairway. "How about these two bags?" I ask. "They'll fit in the overhead rack above your seat," the conductor answers.

He's a young conductor, wearing the years old, maybe centuries old, dark navy uniform and squared conductor's cap. He's impersonal but polite. He makes no offer to help with luggage, mine or the other boarding passengers, all of us seniors.

Small lights mounted low illuminate the aisle. I pass human forms assembled on double seats covered with quilts, blankets, coats. The conductor leads me to an empty double seat on the south side of the train heading west. The seat has generous leg room, more than first class air travel. The car is clean, non-smoking, and comfortably heated. I take my seat and study the controls—lights, backrest and footrest adjustments. The conductor returns with two pillows, one for me and one for my fellow Staples boarding passenger. She has brought her own full-sized pillow and tosses her train pillow to me.

The train pulls out of Staples. I negotiate my four by four foot space, trying for a reclined position of relative comfort. Other passengers look snug and comfortable, press-fit into their seats. Snow falls, and I glance at the white night outside and recognize Verndale, then Wadena with the Super One sign lighting fresh snow in a car-less parking lot. I stay awake and watch rural Wadena County slip into rural Otter Tail.

The scenery is flat, monochromatic, lifeless. A yard light burns yellow in a distant farm yard. A faint light shines through a barn window in another. We travel parallel to Highway 10. Motor traffic is light and heads east, opposite the train's direction. We overtake a semi, aglitter with running lights, then a car. The motion of the train stirs the snow on the rail bed, and, all the while, the quiet click of wheels over weldments compliments the gentle sway of the car. Through the window across the aisle, I recognize Perham and Frazee. We slow to our first stop at Detroit Lakes.

I study the sleeping arrangements of my neighbors in the light of the DL depot, and note that the seats include leg rests. Once they are raised, I negotiate a sleeping space. I remove my shoes, wind my body into a fetal position, and sleep to the rocking motion, waking as we slow for the stop at Fargo.

I stay awake now and observe bleakness of the Dakota prairie. Flat white space, treeless, unfenced, uninhabited. The only signs of settlement are utility poles beside the tracks, their wires gently arced. An east bound freight train roars past my window. Double deck boxcars follow flat cars to create brief flashes of light, like a strobe. I settle down to sleep, and it works. I wake to the loud speaker announcing first call to breakfast.

Mealtime on a train is an opportunity to mingle. Tables seat four passengers, and if there is a table with three diners, a lone diner is seated with them. The camaraderie is instant. Where are you going? Where are you from? Have you ridden the train before? Pity the people who want a quiet breakfast. Not on the Empire Builder.

The morning wears into noon and then afternoon. We are in western North Dakota. Ragtag fences outline small corrals. Grain bins stand in proud formation. John Deere Green adorns snowy white yards. Beside impressive investments of farm equipment stands a modest house, one story, weathered paint, tack-on porch. Herefords pick at hay spread in the corral. Saddle horses stand on the south side of the barn.

In late afternoon, the Montana foothills are sunbathed to a tawny suede. My dinner partner is from Montana. She says that the state population is less than 900,000. My other dinner partner, from Chicago, says gosh, we have more people than that in the Sears Tower.

We stop at Cut Bank, Montana. The train blocks Main Street, north and south. Cars and trucks stack up while the railroad crossing signals flash. I turn away to avoid angry stares of drivers.

We cross the Cut Bank River on a tall, unseen trestle. The landscape is barren but fascinating. Now and then, a graveyard of retired combines, toppled house trailers, a rusty '39 Ford nosed into a scrap heap. Monolithic grain elevators, Peavey and Farmers Co-op. Fat Albert silos of belted, corrugated steel. Three deer feeding near the tracks look like lawn ornaments. Oil derricks outside Cut Bank pump to a steady, monotonous tempo.

Montana is undulating hills of alternate plowed and unplowed patches, like a checkerboard. A string of Black Angus cattle feeds on a trail of hay. A straggler cow licks her newborn calf. Pheasants scratch near the tracks. Quail fly and glide, fly and glide, past the window. More scrap piles—cars, appliances, snarls of barbed wire burned to a shiny blue black. Scraps of orange plastic snag on a fence post and wave as we pass.

It's dark when we eat dinner at East Glacier Park, Montana. Snow falls, and depot lights illuminate spruce trees lathered in white. The scene looks like a movie set. Two more stops before my destination, Whitefish, Montana. Purpose: to ski Big Mountain. The snow jumpstarts my adrenalin. We arrive at Whitefish at 9:15 P.M., on schedule.

For a traveler accustomed to flying, the train is a step back. Way back. Chalk it up to an experience, if time is not an issue, or you want variety. It's hard to imagine that train travel will survive; Amtrak is not a money maker. But it has a charm and simplicity of earlier times. The call of the whistle. The gentle rock of the cars. The easy conversation in the club car. The smell of roast beef from the dining car. The panorama outside the window—farms turning into prairies, turning into foothills, turning into mountains.

Incidentally, the skiing was great.

Poetry

by Cynthia Ekren

Lost Connection

Her phone number
never memorized,
seldom dialed.
Though the
voice is familiar,
the message has changed—messenger has changed.
Phones are smaller,
distance growing by the hour, minute, second,
recorded on monthly bills.

No way to reach so far back
to the long blizzard days singing to our records at the top
of our lungs.
Hot summer nights sleeping out in the back yard with
the black dog for protection.
No calling back to the single heart
that loved and hated me
more than anyone else will love and hate me.
Knowing her heart and my heart
don't recognize our new rhythm beating out of sync.
No phone conversation
can tap it out.
Those girls are
old recordings, distorted
a reminder of something
left behind.

Poetry – Honorable Mention
by Luke Anderson

The Old Fence Row

Years ago, these oak posts were set by the hand
of settlers claiming rights to this tall grass prairie.
It was the boundary to their virgin homestead land
and the livestock could not wander far away,
kept behind three tiers of barbed wire strands.

Today, there remains only grey weathered sticks
protruding askew from the wild and weedy row.
A snarl of barbed wire with sharp metal pricks
guards a meadowlark's nest in grass below,
and the pocket gopher diggings lay thick.

Tomorrow, they'll rip out this old fence row,
since they cultivate land on both sides of it.
They'll come with a thirty-foot digger in tow,
and fret that extra turns grind away the profit
and impede the pace of the field work flow.

Fiction – Honorable Mention

by Kathleen Free

Faded Images

Frank tinkered with the umbrella lights, checked his light meter, and adjusted the backdrop. Sam, his only grandson, will ship out to Iraq next week. These may be the last photographs, he thought. His throat tightened as he fought tears.

"I'm ready, Gramps," Sam said to Frank.

"I'm not," Frank said; his voice faltered. He turned toward Sam. "Take one step forward."

Wearing desert fatigues, Sam stepped toward Frank, stood erect, shoulders back, proud in the glare of light aimed at his face. Tall, bronzed, tough. He held his helmet under his right arm, black boots laced tight, a toothy grin on his face.

"How's this?"

"Perfect." Frank snapped the photograph. "When I get back, I'll sure have some stories to tell," said Sam. "You never told me about your days in the Guard. You got any stories?"

"Nope," said Frank.

"That's because you were in the Guard and not the Marines."

* * *

Friday, May 1, 1970, the day after Nixon announced the invasion of Cambodia by U.S. troops, expanding the Vietnam War, storms of protest began across the country. Near the college campus, fiery speeches turned into bonfires on city streets. By Saturday night, the hostilities blew into a holocaust of fear and hate; students burned the wooden ROTC building; the National Guard arrived.

* * *

Frank dragged the lights backward, setting them for a

new pose. "I'll take a couple of you sitting, without the flag in the background."

"Okay. How about I crouch on one knee? Leave the flag though, Gramps."

The flag. Frank wasn't sure how he felt about the flag. But Sam wanted it in the picture.

"You know, I was thinking, when you get out, you could take over for me here at the studio," Frank said. "I'm ready to retire."

"We've been over this," Sam interrupted, sounding like a parent to his grandfather's little-boy request. "I'm a Marine."

"Okay." Frank knew working with the mundane details of professional photography would not satisfy Sam, yet. "Why don't you wait until you come back to make any decisions about your future?"

"I already know what I want. But if it makes you feel better, I'll wait 'til I get back, and then I'll tell you the same thing again." Sam chuckled and shook his head.

"That makes me feel better," said Frank, trying to contain the sarcasm that dripped inside his mouth. "Which do you think is your best side?"

"My backside," Sam quipped.

Frank chuckled. "Try looking to the right."

"Would that be my right or your right, sir?"

"Your right."

Sam snapped his attention right, his jaw aligned over his shoulder.

"Not that far right. Did you hurt your neck?" asked Frank. But his question floated unanswered, as Sam's imagination soared.

"How's this? I'm looking off in the distance. I see the insurgents. They're coming. Our guys are moving into position. We're sure to take them now. We're smarter, our weapons far superior."

* * *

Frank could name the month, the day, and the exact hour Sam's dreams of glory, his obsession with being a hero, and his unquestioning patriotism began: 6:30 P.M., September 14, 1993. Sam's seventh birthday. Frank's son Dale, Sam's father, had given Sam a child-sized black plastic gun, green fatigues, and a helmet. Frank had questioned the appropriateness of a military uniform for a young boy. But Dale had smiled and said, "The boy needs something fun in his life. What does he have? No mother, since she ran off; me, I'm busy all day at the warehouse; and an old lady to come home to after school."

Frank was about to suggest football or coin collecting, when Sam slammed out the door, replete with helmet, fatigues, gun, and wearing his old cowboy boots. The older men watched as the little boy strutted across the yard, hid behind the bushes in front of the garage, and aimed at the neighbor's calico cat. "Pow, pow, pow," yelled Sam. The cat bolted up the nearest tree. Sam's face shone with excitement. "Whoa," he cried, throwing his arms in the air and waving the gun.

"You know I was in the Guard, but you don't know the story," whispered Frank.

"You were doing your duty," interrupted Dale.

"My duty?" Frank's eyebrows shot up.

"My son is not going to be a pansy-ass." Dale threw the words at Frank. "Good shot, son," he called to Sam.

* * *

Sunday, May 3, the tension between students and Guardsmen lurked in drifting currents, just below the surface. Frank stood at the top of a small hill overlooking an open grassy area called the Commons. His M1 rifle was slung over his left shoulder. Last night he had used his tear gas for the first time. Last night, under orders, he had affixed his bayonet.

A girl, wearing jeans, sandals, a tie-dyed tee shirt, with sweatshirt arms tied around her waist, strode up to Frank.

"Hello, soldier," she said. "Bum a cancer stick from ya?"

"I don't smoke," said Frank.

"You don't want to be here, do you?"

"No, I've got a six-year-old son at home, so I really don't want to be here."

"I can dig that. I think the rally tomorrow will be the last of the protest, until next weekend."

"I thought tomorrow's rally was banned," Frank said.

"I know. If it goes down, you won't kill me, will you?"

"Of course not. The gun is only for intimidation."

"I hope so." Under the girl's cool attitude hid a shadow of fear.

"We're here to keep the peace." Frank tried to reassure her.

"Yeah," she said, looking at the M1. "I'll pray for you." She sounded sincere.

"Pray for me?" Frank was incredulous.

"Yeah, man. We *all* need help to get through this."

The girl turned and sauntered back down the hill.

"You be careful," Frank called after her.

The girl turned and waved.

* * *

Monday, May 4, the rally begins shortly before noon. More than three thousand people fill the Commons area: demonstrators, cheering spectators, and passive onlookers. One hundred National Guardsmen stand watch.

Frank looks out over a peaceful sea of young people. The general gives the order for the demonstrators to disperse. Frank watches as news of the order blows angry waves upon the sea of students. A few of the students throw rocks and hurl a torrent of obscenities at the Guardsmen. The general orders his men to load and lock their weapons. Frank loads a clip. The general orders the Guard to march across the Commons and disperse the crowd. Frank fires tear gas into the crowd. The sea recoils, as if a freezing wind has blown it toward an opposite shore. The Guardsmen follow. The demonstrators pull back to a football field. Again the Guardsmen follow, but within minutes they feel trapped by the surrounding fence. Frank feels fear for the first time. Some Guardsmen kneel and point their weapons. Frank pulls his rifle off his shoulder. The Guardsmen retreat to the same small hill, where yesterday Frank had chatted with the girl. The sea follows; the tide has turned.

Yesterday seems so far away, Frank is thinking when he hears shots from behind him. He spins around. Almost half the Guardsmen are firing; a few fire into the sea of people. Frank fires his weapon into the air, into the air, into the air. He's afraid. He might fire into the people. God help me, he prays. The shooting stops.

Only thirteen seconds have passed. Four young people are dead; nine lay injured.

* * *

"I think we're finished here," Frank said to Sam. "Unless you want me to take a few shots outdoors."

"Nah, these will be great," said Sam. "Can you make copies of the good ones?"

"Sure," said Frank.

"And the newspaper will need a black and white photo," said Sam, from the changing room.

"Okay. I'll see they get it." Frank mumbles, "Funny, the media always reports life in black and white, when it's lived in shades of gray."

"Gramps," said Sam, now dressed in civilian clothes. "Since this may be the last time we're alone . . . " Sam stopped.

"What?" asked Frank.

"If anything happens to me, take care of Dad."

"Okay." Frank grabbed Sam and hugged him. "Don't let anything happen to you, Sam."

"I'm going to do my best," said Sam. "And when I get back, I might write a book, filled with the stories of my adventures."

"I hope you do," said Frank. "It's the stories you *don't* tell that will haunt you for the rest of your life."

Poetry – Honorable Mention

by Larry Schug

Dirty Hands

Grease and machine oil
fill the cracks in my fingers
and the palms of my hands.
At break time and lunch time
I scrub my hands
with a stiff-bristled brush
and pink hand-cleaner from the dispenser
above the slop sink,
make my hands clean enough
to eat a doughnut and a sandwich,
but not clean enough for making love.

At home, I scrub them again
with gritty green soap and a scouring pad.
Even after a hot water soaking,
my hands, white and wrinkled, appear clean,
but when dry, I can still see ground-in grease
deep in the cracks of my skin;
and I think my hands will never be clean,
any more than the words in my head
will ever be cleaned into poetry,
no matter how many times
I drag them across a new page.

Poetry

by Linda M. Johnson

Shelves of Memory

My old bookcase isn't an heirloom or antique,
its monetary value next to nothing.
It's simply old.
The wood is easily scratched, the finish dark.
Shelves are slim, with only three of them
it stands barely heart-high.

It came from my childhood home
where it sat proudly in the living room holding Mom's books.
The one I remember was a thick, blue and white volume
titled "*History of the Finns in Minnesota.*"

Mom was smart; everyone said so.

I don't remember smart.
I remember hot chocolate with buttered toast,
knowing she would be there when I got off the bus.
My sense of security changed the first day back at school
after the funeral.

The bookcase now stands in my bedroom
where I keep books of poetry, a Bible, Mom's picture.
Yet no matter what words lie on those shelves,
the bookcase knows my story.

Poetry
by Jodi Buchan

Transplant

I squint toward the past
Gather the strength of graves,
See in the rising and setting and rising of sun
Hills echoing a familiar song on distant shores a lofty sail away
And I have an ache, a longing for clover-touched fingertips.

Caressing verdant paper pastures, I envision her embrace
The kiss of her warm earth in the still of my dream
Where I tilt my face to her breath,
A wind that breaks off the crescents of waves,
Rises up rocky cliffs and climbs over field,
Seeping into the lungs of my forefathers,
Who do not gasp against the bracing blue gray—
But swallow it whole, drink in the dank elixir
Until they tremble with salt stung eyes,
Seek refuge within their thatched cottages:
Damp peat smoking, soda bread baking, raised glasses toasting,
Voices lifting above the chink of rain falling upon their cornerstones.

I bend my ear toward the past
Gather the strength of graves,
Listen to the rising and falling and rising of shadows
Place their songs in my distant breast where I have an ache,
A longing for a mother's clover-touched lips.

Poetry – Honorable Mention

by Thomas C. Stetzler

Last House on the Road

I am a house of unfinished rooms
  boarded up windows
unframed doors
  Ghosts of men off the highway
take shelter here
  Perhaps they rise from deep soil
like reluctant moles
  surfacing from mad
subterranean journeys

One traveler curled up here
  on a sub-zero night
and
  his cheap bottle of medicine drained
scrawled upon the crude wooden wall
  in his last hour of warmth
eloquent lines of epitaph
  then met the sunrise
laid out in a gown of snow

Poetry

John H. Thornberg

Vigil

Five-thirty in the morning,
sleep must be on standby
and missed its connection.
The thin blade of first light
is working its way up the dark
stubbled chin of the planet
barely mirrored in the basin
that cradles my peaceful lake.
The long transatlantic flight
of a new day arrives on time
and I am nodding at the gate
already making plans to find
it a nice quiet place to rest.

Creative Nonfiction – Honorable Mention
by Lorna Rafness

Montana Roads

My mother informed me that I was going to Montana, whether I wanted to or not.

In 1955, after graduating from high school, my sister Midge took a job at a resort near Red Lodge. Family friends owned the place and it was decided that my parents would drive out to pick her up at the end of the season. One might expect that life was dull in my small home-town of Minneota, in southwestern Minnesota. But as a teenager, I had managed to find ways to make it exciting. And certainly, I didn't want to leave the boy who was currently assisting me in that endeavor. I was the youngest of four kids, and my parents largely left me to my own devices. They were not major players in my scheme of things and the idea of going on a trip with them, anywhere at all, was the worst and dullest thing I could think of. However, it was no use to resist. I knew persuasion, lies, and whining would all be futile, thus demeaning for me. My mother seldom interfered in my life but when she did, I had to accept it.

Pauline Fox, a friend of Midge's, was invited along for the ride. Neither of us had ventured far from Minneota and Pauline, the nineteenth child in a family of twenty kids, had fewer opportunities than most. She was a fun-loving and lively seventeen-year-old, but she was also a dedicated Roman Catholic with aspirations of becoming a nun. I had just passed my fifteenth birthday and was a rebellious teenager with nothing much to rebel against. My parents were easygoing and wrapped up in their own lives. So I got a big kick out of the attention Pauline gave me. She was easily shocked by my boisterous behavior and language (use of the F-word, and every other swear-word I could think of). For one thing, I tried to convince her that a case could be made for legalizing prostitution, maybe even elevating it to an honorable profession. I forget what the positive points of my argument were. I also embellished on some stories about my risky behavior with boys. It was true that my friends and I frequently allowed ourselves to be picked up—confident in the boys' harmless intentions. Pick-ups could provide interesting adventures. Pauline, however, would not be persuaded that it was a good way to make new friends.

We spent two nights in motels on the drive to Montana and my parents bedded down early, leaving Pauline and me to entertain ourselves. We would stroll around town, and that's when I got the chance to show off for her, smoking contraband cigarettes, swearing and trying to flirt with the few boys we encountered. If she hadn't been so receptive and amused by me, I wouldn't have opened up to her at all. I would have played my silent self, feeling as though I were imprisoned by aliens, but because of her I enjoyed myself.

Once we got to the resort, I had an even better time. My poor mother got carsick on the last leg of the trip, so when we got there she had to recuperate. That gave my dad the opportunity to indulge himself in the forbidden pleasures of the bar-room: forbidden to him by my mother because he had proven himself incapable of moderation. With both my parents preoccupied, Pauline, my sister, and I were on our own. The first night when the three of us walked into the dance-hall, I had a good-looking guy winking at me within minutes (without my glasses they were all good-looking). I wasn't practiced at winking so I raised one eyebrow and tried to look like my idea of sexy sophistication. I'd seen a friend of mine practice this in front of a mirror and it looked good on her. It must have worked because soon my winking friend was my dancing partner while Midge and Pauline were involved in mild flirtations of their own. As we danced together, he commented that I had come-hither eyes and I made a mental note to keep the one-raised-eyebrow technique as part of my repertoire. Then I wondered whether he was making fun of me—but decided I didn't care. After all, he *was* out on the dance floor with me.

We stayed at the resort three nights. Most of my time was spent with the winker on his motorcycle. I don't remember much about him, not even his name, just the rides he took me on. It was my first time on a bike and all I knew was that speeding around in the winding mountainous terrain was breathtaking. At fifteen, we think we're immortal, but I did feel—*almost*—afraid a few times on those rides. My parents had no idea I was out alone with a guy on a motorcycle. They supposed I was spending my time with Midge and Pauline. Midge didn't know the guy well and she didn't like it when I left with him, but she couldn't do anything about it and she was never a tattletale.

Once again, I had lucked out and picked a nice guy or I might have been in big trouble. He must have been old enough to drink legally, and when he offered me beer, I just sipped on his. I had learned to respect alcohol and the time and place for me to indulge was not alone with a stranger in a strange place. My need for risk-taking was sufficiently reinforced just by hanging out with a leather-clad, handsome, beer-drinking biker. And smoking with him—that is the ordinary-cigarette kind of smoke. In my small-town experience of the 1950s, I had read about smoking pot, better known as reefer at the time, but that only happened in New York City or Mexico or exotic places like that. And it was dangerous; one puff and you were hooked, and your brain rotted, or fried, or some such thing.

I think my biker friend knew I was younger than I pretended to be, and there in Montana, the nights were cold, not conducive to long-term making-out in the great outdoors. Apparently understanding my relative innocence, he was satisfied with dancing, necking, and the bike rides on those treacherous roads. No doubt what he enjoyed most was riding his Harley and pushing his driving limits. Testing himself to see how fast he could take those curves with me hanging on to him for dear life. And testing me to see how much I could take before crying out in fear. In my naivety, I had complete trust in his ability to master his machine against all odds, and only loosed the occasional instinctive gasp besides involuntarily tightening my already intense grip around his waist.

In the meantime, Midge was occupied with planning for a future with her boyfriend stationed in Norfolk, Virginia. And although Pauline told me she appreciated my viewpoint, her nunnish characteristics nevertheless outweighed her party-girl tendencies and she did go on to enter a convent. Inevitably, my time for fun and games soon ran out. Reality set in and it became clear to me that my life wasn't going anywhere. So I just gave up. Giving up led to the mommy-track for me before I turned seventeen.

Poetry
by Sharon Harris

Yearning

I sit in a coffee shop,
alone
but not by choice,

missing you
and not far enough
from funeral arrangements
to remember just the good things,

feeling my age,
while steam
drifts up from my cup.

idly I watch
as a young boy
comes in with his girl.

they are new to each other,
I can tell,
unsure what to say
and how to say it,
blushing but smiling
broadly at each other.

oh, to be that young,
to have it all start again—
that first blush of love,
the promise
of a whole long life
still ahead of us.

Poetry
by Rosa Carlisle

Mama Paints Her Fingernails

before the bridge party
blowing me a bedtime kiss
warning me not to touch

I miss her scented hands
sweet with perfume
brushing through my hair
touching my waiting face

nightmares haunt me
plates falling jam spilling
chipped red fingernails
stained doeskin gloves

I awaken to her fingers
waving goodbye to me
ruby red nails hiding
in white doeskin gloves

I dress in Mama's clothes
sending my dolls to bed
without a tea party
or bedtime kisses

the first day in school
mothers hug their children
wiping away their tears
with naked hands

I hold tightly to
doeskin gloves

Poetry
by Roy C. Booth

The Intangible Discourse

On a sunny playground
Two swings
Sway companionably,
As if a pair of ghosts
Sit talking quietly,
Swinging to and fro,
About times long past
And the weather,
Listening to the breeze,
And the laughter of children
As a distant strum of music is heard
Through the flickering leaf shade.

Fiction
by William Schmitt

Atta Boy

Fricken eh, they're walking past me and queuing up at the coffin like the Pope himself is lying in state. They pay their respects, but they didn't pay the price of living with the son of a bitch. Our family put the D in dysfunctional, but then, hey, cry me a river; we all have ghosts in our closets.

Early on, it was just spankings, which graduated into the use of a wide belt across the rear end while my age was still in the single digits. After that, it was slapping the face, which was around the time he started to work out of town and only came home on the weekends to police the past week's activities. During my teens, it matured into a fist to the gut, generally after plenty of "barley pop" and some good old whiskey to balance things out. Anyway, such was the nurturing treatment for the boys; the girls had their own issues.

I suppose it was inevitable, coming home on the weekends changed to every other weekend, then eventually not at all. Finally, it came to a head with divorce between the folks. That's fine; they weren't getting it on and why prolong the suffering. The son of a bitch always preached "cut your losses and move on." I guess he finally did.

But there was that one time we went fishing up in Canada. I was in my early teens or thereabout and the old man and I were sitting in a boat tucked in a back bay up against the woods and wild. It was early afternoon on one of those precious June days where the sun was warm, the humidity low, and the bugs absent. The boat was motionless, for the lake was like blue glass and the clear sky was spotted with white cotton balls, to the extent that when you looked down lake you couldn't tell where the sky began and the lake ended.

We were flogging the water not so much to catch fish, but more to inhale the tranquility of Mother Nature and to get lost in our thoughts. The old man was at his best in times like these. Always an avid outdoorsman, he found solitude and himself in the wilderness.

Slow to retrieve my lure after casting it out, I paid the price of getting it snagged on the bottom. So while I reeled up the slack line, the old man maneuvered the boat with an oar until we were directly over the lure, which was still holding tight to the bottom. Increasing my grip on the rod tugs to free the lure below, it startled me when the monofilament popped and my pole went straight.

Instantly, we both looked over the side of the boat into the indigo depths and there below us was a twinkle on the bottom. We gasped as we each acknowledged the distant lure. As we stared at this speckle far below, the old man asked what I was using. I said a Mepps #3 bucktail spinner.

"Really? The one you have been catching all the fish on?"

"Yup, that's it."

"Oh, Baby, we got to do something."

Now I've been around him long enough to know that "we" generally means me. But I was amused, so I bit on his line and asked, "What have you got in mind?"

"How about you take off your clothes and dive in after that lure? Your killer Mepps spinner is laying down there waiting to be rescued."

Chuckling lightly, I said, "Why don't you take off your clothes and dive in after it?" Well, I should have seen it coming, for he immediately launched into his "Navy" spiel about how he served in the Great War aboard a submarine for four years and, being the senior officer, it was his duty to stay with the ship . . . blah, blah, blah.

OK—OK, I knew I wasn't going to win that one, but I wasn't yet totally convinced. So I asked him how deep he thinks it is where the lure is hung up.

He scoffed at my question and replied, "Not deep at all, maybe two or three fathoms at most." (He always played the Navy/nautical thing when on a boat.) I'm thinking to myself, hey, that's not bad, I can dive a couple fathoms. Soon I was to learn that one fathom is about thirty feet!

Anyway, at the time it seemed like a good idea. So I strip down and step off the side of the boat into the pristine Canadian waters, which I instantly realize is a huge mistake. Now you have to remember, this is Canada in late June, which means the ice went out on the lake, oh—last week. My breath escaped me and my skin turned a pale shade of blue as my testicles sucked up into my body cavity. Then and there, I should have auditioned for the Vienna Boys choir!

So I'm clinging for life onto the side of the boat attempting to catch my breath and wondering what the heck I got myself into. Dad is above me in the boat egging me on with, "Are you ready—are you ready? I can still see the lure shining on the bottom."

Inhaling a big breath, I head for the bottom. Now it's different diving without a mask; things are not as clear. So when I reach bottom I'm doing more feeling than seeing, even though I can still see a dimmer twinkle. But I can't connect with it and, after my oxygen runs out, I head towards the surface.

As soon as I break the water's surface, Dad asks, "You got it?"

Gasping to get some air, I respond with a shallow, "No."

"We'll get it this time," he says. "Hurry up—hurry up, get back down there."

After a couple more deep breaths, I head back down. Again, I'm fumbling on the bottom and running out of air. I just can't seem to locate that dang lure, so back to the surface I go.

Instantly, Dad starts in after he realizes I hadn't captured the brass ring. "You can do it—hustle up and get back down there," he encouragingly chants. At this moment, I'm beginning to experience the life of a Japanese pearl diver under the whip of an old samurai.

Once again, I take a couple more deep breaths and head for Davy Jones' Locker. It's totally frustrating for I can still see a glimmer but can't quite pick it up. Since I'm feeling along the bottom, I'm stirring up the silt, which makes things worse. My lungs are burning for oxygen and I'm about to head for the surface when it happened. I found it! Or rather, it found me, for the darn treble hook stuck into my thumb. But I didn't care; I dislodged it from the rocks and kicked for the surface.

Breaking out of the water, I shout, "I got it!"

Immediately Dad screams back . . . "Atta Boy!" which is the

holy grail of compliments for us kids. Whether it was catching that fly ball, getting a B on the report card, or cutting the grass without being told, when you got an "Atta Boy," you were on top of your game.

Dad said to come around to the stern of the boat (more nautical stuff) and he would help me in. He pulls me up by the motor and I work my way toward the front of the boat. I sit in the bow seat and, bursting with pride, I ceremoniously lay the Mepps spinner on the empty seat between us. Letting the sun dissolve the goose bumps, feeling my testicles recede, and having blood return to my skin all felt really good, but not as good as getting an "Atta Boy."

Looking over at Dad, I notice that he has an ear to ear grin on his face. Like the saying goes, when you're invited to a poker game and you can't recognized the sucker, then it must be you. "So, tell me, Dad, would you have jumped in after your lure?"

"Hell, no," he bellows. "Not for a nickel lure and besides I have four more of them exact lures in my tackle box." We both cackle and howl. But really, the laugh wasn't on me as much as the laugh was between us.

Now the son of a bitch is stiff as a board and I'm not going to take a look. He wasn't around enough when I was young and he's not here now. Next weekend I'm hauling his sorry ass (ashes) up North to our hunting shack, where we spent the last twenty years chasing deer and grouse. I promised him I would spread him out up there. But what bothers me most is that I never got to tell him how much I liked fishing.

Poetry

by Richard G. Hagen

Struck by an Image

I

Smack in the back
Down on his face
Dirt in the eyes
Inhale of sand
Move move move move
Get around truck
Straighten up, aim
Return fire
Feel slamming pain
From that impact.
Yell, others down?
Yell, is there blood?
Grip on weapon
Weaker now.
God that hurt.
Plates in armor
Split by the slug.
Adrenalin
Slowing now
Pain increases
Stiffness begins
As does anger
Realization
No wound.
Lucky day.

II

The image will ever be with me.
Seeing him from behind,
From a distance, faceless,
Not hearing the shot,
Forced forward, arms out,
Face down, feet off the earth.
All a father's memories
Of his boy, fixed forever
In the man's voice
On the cell phone,
Saying to me, "Don't
Worry, Dad, it's
Cool now. Just stiff."
Too shook to tell me,
Too proud to brag,
He told me about it on Easter,
Although it took place
Weeks before. Praise God
To learn of a son
Rising from death
That day.

Poetry

by Tracy Gulliver

Inquisition

Too many times
You demanded to know
What was wrong with me.
Why did I insist
on making your life so difficult?

And I probed every crevice
of my soul, trying
to come up with an adequate answer,
never having time to consider
there might be something wrong
with the question.

Poetry
by Cynthia Ekren

The Chair

(for Linda and Keith)

The lovely leather chair
he brought from his city condo
to her earth home up north
            changed
her life.
The supple strength of the dark brown cushions,
rich mahogany of the arms
signaled the fate of the worn purple couch
where her former mate
drank and slept.

They clashed.

When she first became enfolded in the chair's
grandeur in the sun-filled room,
the chair commanded all ugliness
trashed or sold away.

She saw how her fine art posters come
full color

Now that they were lit from above.

Fiction

by Laura L. Hansen

The Picture; A Flash Fiction

How typical that I can't see the whole picture. You walk away through the dark slit of door, leaving the pictures we bought together un-hung and letting the dog out without a leash. I see his muscular white body leaping away across the poorly lit street. He looks elated to be free of the gloom, to be free of us. I can't even mourn his betrayal, seeing him leap across the curb and dash away. God speed, I think, and turn to see the tip of your sleeve—your favorite gray wool jacket—slip out of view and into the car.

I settle by the window with the newspaper, losing myself in other people's lives. Despite your leaving, your things—our things—still clutter the floor and remain stacked up against walls. Already you exist in my mind like a partial picture, the kind where someone aims the camera wrong and when you go to pick up the pictures and open the envelope (all full of expectation), you see a body, a sweater, a pair of pale and slightly dry hands, but no head. That is how I view us now. The picture I thought we had taken is not the picture I hold in my hand.

Poetry
by Marion C. Holtey

Mother's Meditation

I dip crusts of bread into
a dish of slippery olive oil
surrounded by an island
of dark balsamic vinegar.

Remembering things past
the odor of olive oil floats
across my mind as it drifted
over her quiet retreat.

She sat at the kitchen table
one hand draped into a bowl
of warm oil, the late August
sun turning it to pale gold.

Another hand held a wooden stick
poised to push back the cuticle as
her head nodded to strains of Brahms
from the new Hi-Fi in the living room.

A private time stolen from daily
duties as housewife and mother
she escaped to nourish her soul
in quiet moments of meditation.

Poetry – Editor's Choice

by Margaret Hasse

When Soda Always Came in Glass Bottles

Glass pop bottles glint in a Dakota ditch,
worth money if picked up intact, delivered
in town to a small store where a pop machine
shaped like a heavy box with a see-through lid
is so deep a thirsty child must rest her tummy
on the edge like a fulcrum, her fanny up,
to reach way down into icy water
and slide a new bottle along metal bars
like stanchions that secure the heads of cows.

Such choices there: Nehi orange and grape,
the green of Squirt, and the earthy amber
of what the Methodist youth leaders
call not root beer but *rootsie pop*—
the word *beer* forbidden,
as are cigarettes, even candy ones
with their lit ends pansy pink,
and also lipstick and the kohl of makeup
that enlarge and darken bad girls' eyes.

At the back of the store, faceless men
hunch like buffalo over girlie magazines,
savoring sweets they don't want to share
with the young girl who's old enough
to feel squirmy, sensing that what's enjoyed
has something to do with her braided hair,
pretty freckled face, and the changes
her body's beginning to show, public
as a parade coming right down Main Street.

Poetry

by Penelope Swan

Even Then The Poet Was In Me

Before my new sister came home from the hospital my pet rabbit Petey was banished, his teeth marks fresh on the vacuum's cord. They gave me a hairless doll with unblinking eyes; its head stinking of rubber.

I wanted a live, furry thing, a heart thumping in my palm.

So I began the cutting in my parents' bedroom, taking my time snipping edges of floor length drapes, dallying over stems of blues and cremes, petals of pinks and maroons until contortions of ruin sprawled in piles mouthing

what my child's mind could not say.

Laboring on, I shaped lavish holes in the taut belly of the bed's spread

pulling through the pink-skinned sheet.

But it was those last cuts I savored most. In the dark of their closet I hacked at my straight, virgin hair skiving a bald spot dead center.
Held my finger

on its pulse.

When called into the living room to gaze into the fancy bassinet set up for visitors cooing in awe of lush, dark curls framing my sister's face, I was the only one

who saw beyond perfection.

Bending close to her squashed nose splayed from lip to forehead—no bridge—I pointed to the flat, scripted ***I*** running straight up into her hairline.

What happened here?

No one said. That's the way it is with damage in our family.

Poetry

by Jean Childers

Swimming, backwards

You swam up again and made me laugh.
          I stopped to look where you were.
I crawled away again, and after a few feet,
                    wiggling your head on me to tickle.
          lay on your back, "swimming" up behind me,
You, all happy boy, sturdy jeans, striped shirt and simple joys of
   youth,
          I crawled away from you.
Me, all chubby and short dark curls and open-mouthed determination
   in my rubber pants,
                    (linoleum in those days, remember?)
          you chased me around the living room floor
Back when buzz cuts were popular the first time around,
Me . . . toddler, you . . . 9 or 10.
          films of my youth and your innocence.
No sound, but grainy colors, those
The whirr of the 8mm projector echoes off the paneled walls.

Fiction
by Susan K. Spindler

Sarah

He was ugly. There was just no other way to describe him. Too tall, which gave him the appearance of hovering, too gangly: ditto. Too creepy, that having nothing to do with the length of the legs. And those John Lennon glasses! Oh, please! What did her mother see in him? Eric, quintessential librarian. Wine connoisseur extraordinaire. Are you kidding me? Sarah found herself asking her mother that question often and heatedly. And, a second question: "Mother, are you out of your mind?!" Mind, however, was something Sarah knew her mother, tenured physics professor, did not lack.

Sarah, attempting to outsmart, plotted and fumed, followed her mother's suggestion that they all go to the zoo together. Act nice to him, Sarah told herself. Follow the two of them to the dorky zoo on a nice maybe-we-can-be-a-threesome outing. Pretend to have fun. Take a picture of him next to the tall-but-dumb giraffes, the bull moose with the gargantuan ears, dull as a plank. Perfect! Mother, would you see the resemblances? Would you get it then?

But no, her mother did not. This inflamed Sarah, as did her mother's patience. She did not succumb to reciprocal screaming, up-the-ante sarcasm, tirades invoking past injustice, despite Sarah's best attempts at provocation. Instead, she would listen, say how sad she was and that she hoped Sarah could one day accept Eric.

What absolute crap! Why wouldn't she fight back? And why, when her mother refused to fight, did Sarah feel terrified, as if ice filled her heart, leaving her cold and shaking? Was this a battle between Sarah and her mom, or an active attempt to destroy her mother's happiness? Could it really be that? How ridiculous! Her friend Jennie asked, "Sarah, don't you want your Mom to be happy?" Sarah noticed a choking sensation in the back of her throat. Her retort stuck there without release.

Not that the battle plan was restricted to giraffes and moose. There was the time Sarah backed the car out of the garage, took the side mirror off his prissy turquoise shouldn't-have-been-setting-in-our-driveway-in-the-first-place Ford Taurus. Who would be stupid enough to get a turquoise car? But, what a perfect chance to observe him, losing it in front of her mother. She remembered being aghast at his words: "I appreciate your telling me, Sarah. I know that took courage." Oh. My. Gosh. Did he think she didn't see through that? What kind of a man could be so afraid of a fifteen-year-old? Where was his anger?

Or the time Eric and her mother had planned a romantic night on a St. Croix riverboat. Sarah, by happenchance, got really constipated that night. It came on suddenly. Nothing she could have predicted. Surprisingly, it became painful so quickly. Cramps like a battering ram rumbling toward Gibraltar. It certainly was not her wish to have had to call her mother and Eric on their way to Stillwater, to have had to tearfully plead, cajole, bleat, that they help her. "Please, Mom, we are out of Ducolax. I tried Dad already. He's not home. Mom, help me." Certainly, they would know that she couldn't have planned this.

Sarah couldn't have known, of course, that more than once this archrival, this cold dork with the beady green eyes whom she hated, posed a question to her mother: "How long do you think you can face the pain your daughter is in because of me?" Sarah also did not know her mother's response, "Eric, I'm not going anywhere. I don't think this is about you." And she did not know that her mother pondered his tolerance for standing exposed on the firing range of her angry teenage daughter.

When Sarah's mother sought to understand her anger, Sarah quickly labeled the questions her "what-could-be-wrong-with-Sarah" inquiry. Sarah's fuming about the line of questioning mounted to a relentless broil. Could her mother really believe that all of this energy toward Eric was not about him? What, then, could her dear, smart mother think it was about, if not Eric? Like there's some Gordian Knot mystery about why her daughter had outrage? Hello . . . it is so much like adults to just get so off track and tarry there, wandering around lost in suppositions.

Sarah found herself preoccupied with her mother's inferences, and her own retorts. The two of them built a cadence that was like a tennis match: soft lob to the opponent, powerful overhand back.

"Sarah, I know you don't want me to get hurt again."

"It's kind of you to assume protective thoughts, Mother, but it's not that deep. Honestly, I just can't stand him."

"Sarah, I know that there have been losses for you since your Dad got remarried."

"I get that you are referring to Ms. Torment, stepmother from hell and how Dad has turned to oatmeal in her presence. Mom, I've moved on."

"Sarah, you can't want to spend one more Friday night in your room watching videos. Why don't you invite some friends over?" Sarah felt most humiliated at this last suggestion. Lonely was hard enough to feel. Exposed and lonely was somewhere on top of that, harder, more biting. It bothered her that she was not yet dating and her two best friends were. Nonetheless, better to be watching girl-meets-boy videos than out with a stiff-necked geek like Eric.

Sarah's therapist asked her if she thought it was a good thing that her mother was softening, healing, loving again. The first time she asked, Sarah told her what she thought about the whole line of questioning: "Adults get so preoccupied with things they presume to be true about their troubled children that they miss the truth: sometimes, a parent's choice of a partner is a just plain butt-awful, please-shoot-me-rather-than-make-me-witness-this mistake. Do you need me to say more?" Sarah remembered being startled by her own response. It sounded so defensive. So molten. As if a part of her burned. Hot and wet, like her pillow, when Sarah sobbed into it at night. Alone, confused, and aching. The moment before the gentleness of spent grief released her into the blessed arms of sleep.

Several months later, when her therapist asked the same question a second time, there was this: Sarah could see that her mother was smiling more. The wall of ice and tears that had for so long prickled the battle between her father and her mother was melting. Sarah's mother was now so much more inclined to give Sarah hope and direction in dealing with her stepmother as opposed to tongue-lashing her father. The start of the forgiveness, admittedly, had been Eric. Sarah was sure he would relish the title of He-who-vanquishes-heartache, yet knew that her own heart did not ache twenty-four/seven anymore. Could it be that it was in fact Eric who brought back some of the laughter that Sarah and her mother had lost when her father left?

Even though Sarah had at first reacted to Eric's presence in her mother's life with rage and scorn, she never noticed the developing paradox. As her heart softened to accommodate his presence in her mother's life, he was less present. When he said goodbye to her mother, it left nothing for Sarah to fight against. The void was startling and sudden. For the first time, she saw her mother's pain, apparent in her sleepless nights and reddened eyes.

Sarah pondered the meaning of pain, of heartache. Perhaps heartache has a set mass. It is one huge unshrinkable glob, so that when one heart hurts more, another heart somewhere hurts less. The equation would be x amount of joy = x amount of pain. The two sides always have to be equal. It was an equation based on justice and balance. Her heart had hurt this past year, the hurt of red fury, the hurt of obdurate, dull-beige loneliness and confusion. Her mother, Sarah knew, had fallen in love.

Now it seemed that Sarah's heart should be lightened, relieved, and excited about Eric being gone. But the equation did not align that way this time.

As her mother lost weight and the color of her skin turned a dusky morose, Sarah pondered her mother's assurance that it was not her fault. When Sarah left for a movie, on her first date with a boy, she noted that her heart felt on the sad, empty side of the equation too. Her mother kissed her on the cheek, reminded her of curfew and to drive safely. She watched as the two backed out of the driveway.

The young man at her side was cute, polite, funny. It was good to be going on this long-awaited official start of it all. Sarah looked back at the gaunt figure still in the doorway and wished she could give her mother the life back in her eyes, her half of the joy part of the equation.

Poetry
by Adrian S. Potter
wedding song

my song is
a melodious void from which hunger springs
the unsung ballad inside a wino's bottle
the gutbucket blues of fistfights and failures
an atonal tale of tequila's treacherous hymn
the improvised music of misfortune
as it waits for its opportunity
to break in and steal the moment.

her song is
an unflinching soundtrack that sweetens the air
the singsong double-dutch rhymes of childhood
harmonious bliss found within a sunrise
the tune of teenage truths carved on park benches
a signature lyric loosely based on the storylines
found in dime store romance novels
and made-for-TV movies.

our song is
a testament to the bone-deep ache of desire
the dissonance of two separate winds crossing
a guttural gospel hum of hidden blessings
the unexpected hallelujah of love
envisioned then fully experienced
under God's vigilant eye
as we declare
I do.

Poetry
by Rhoda Jackson

Priya

The Cat basks in the warmth of the sunbeam
Sable limbs stretched,
Sky blue eyes
Softly closed.
Yet brown tipped ears ever alert.

"Feral," they called her.
"Free," said she.

On occasion, the human builds a fire in the wood stove,
She and her feline cousin creep close to bask in the glow.

She and the human have reached an agreement.
The Cat will grace the home with beauty only a feline can possess
And the human may gaze upon her.

But those strange limbs devoid of fur must not,
Not ever,
Touch the Cat.

Creative Nonfiction – Honorable Mention
by Mary Lynn Regnier

Sole Searching

There's nothing to those shoes. Seriously. A dollar's worth of vinyl and a couple of rhinestones. $56.00 . . . on sale! There's no way in this lifetime I would spend that kind of money on shoes like that. At least, I wouldn't if the shoes were for me, but they're not.

I look at her foot so perfectly fitted in those shoes beneath a rolled up pair of faded blue jeans. "They're perfect," she gushes, turning her foot side to side and smiling at the reflection of her ankle in the shoe store mirror.

"They're cheap," I think. "They probably won't last through the dance."

"I can't believe I'm going to the prom," my daughter marvels.

"Neither can I," I silently agree as I look at my baby, who is a baby no more, but rather an orchid which has blossomed overnight and to which you awake one morning and incredulously see in full-bloom. Revelation in a shoe shop.

"They'll be perfect with my dress, Mom," she pleads. "Please, please, please . . . "

Please what? Buy her a pair of cheap shoes or please stand aside as she steps out in the world in rhinestones and silver sandal straps?

"Please!" My Cinderella in blue jeans has found the magic slippers that will take her a few steps farther away from me. I feel old.

"Fine," I sigh, packing the silver slippers back in the cloud of tissue. "We'll take the shoes. You'll be the most beautiful girl at the dance."

"Well, I'll have the most beautiful shoes," she says, stepping back into her beat-up flip-flops.

I pause at the register. I pay $56.00 for the privilege of hiding my heartache.

"Will there be anything else?" the clerk inquires.

"Yes," I sigh. "I could really use some arch supports."

Poetry
by Louise Bottrell

(a little bit of) Immortality

We'd overheard him called rich and eccentric,
but none of us knew him, none had seen him,
and we imagined him sinister, possibly

   no   probably   dangerous. We shivered
in anticipation as we approached the corner
of Vineyard and Vine, whispering and giggling,

sporting siblings' hand-me-down masks,
smelling of moth-balls in make-shift costumes
dredged from trunks and attics and closets.

We clambered up the wooden steps, stumbling
in our too-long trousers or bed sheets wrapping
around our legs, pressed the doorbell, yelled

TRICK OR TREAT and held our breath.
The door creaked open. From the dark recesses
a hand delivered to each of us a folded note:

"This certifies the bearer to receive ONE (1)
ice cream cone from Shafer's Drug Store."
Scrawled across the bottom,
John J. Smyser.

Now here was a treat. In the 1940s, a big deal.
Each Halloween we remember our benefactor
and the enchantment of that paper in our hands.

Poetry
by Traci Nigon

History Class

Though she had never spoken to the boy sitting ten feet away from her, she felt that upon being given the chance, they could talk for moments and minutes and hours, about everything and nothing, until the sun dipped itself below the horizon, until the cool air formed minute droplets of dew upon individual blades in the waves of grass she would run her hands over, until the moon set itself away for another day, and all this would culminate in the exquisite consummation of night as their bodies became as kindred as their souls happened to intrinsically be, and she only thought this because some inexplicable quality in his eyes or demeanor or laughter made her think that maybe they were not so different as they may have seemed.

Poetry
by Toni Bennett Easterson

The Date

The boy across the street
is going to the prom in a black tuxedo.
He poses near a trio of birches
while his mother,
wearing blue jeans,
takes his photograph.

All morning it quietly rained
and when it stopped,
the neighborhood grew
noisy with perennials pushing
and grabbing for space, trees,
recently green, vying for attention.
Now, everything looks new.
The boy stands in a way
he has never stood before;
his mother, looking into the camera,
notices and realizes she, too,
has become a different person.

On the other side of the river a girl,
in a satin charmeuse dress
purchased with money
made working at the Dairy Queen,
slips into strap heels
and waits for Spring.

Fiction
by Jerry Mevissen

Theme and Variations

From the window beside her bed, Lorraine looked out to see a form in a clump of dry leaves. An irregular, oval shape, the size of a scruffy head staring from the Xs and Ys of naked winter branches. Below, snow collected on the patio table and charcoal grill that had remained outside since last summer. Wind cleared the snow on the dome of the grill, leaving the north edge exposed.

"Male pattern baldness," thought Lorraine. "Louie, when will you get out of my life?"

She rose, eager to dispel the image, to shrug off the feelings. She padded to the kitchen, snapped on the radio, and measured coffee grounds. A pot for one, a scrim of familiarity in the solitude.

She surveyed the kitchen, the uncluttered countertops, the empty sink, the bare burners on the stove. Her kitchen now, not Louie's. A week ago, pasta canisters lined the walls. A large ceramic apple cookie jar held biscotti. A popcorn bowl sat in the sink, the unpopped kernels sticking to empty Budweiser cans.

"I don't miss that," she mused. But the stark neutrality of birch cupboards, linen walls, and ivory countertops struck her as a metaphor for her life: orderly, colorless, dull.

"Louie," she thought. "When will you leave me alone?"

Luigi ("call me *Louie*") presented an unexpected attraction when they met. They were different, but she was comfortable in his company. His rough edges contrasted with her well honed manners. His tastes, his talk were unaffected. What first she had perceived as boorish, she later found authentic. And refreshing. As did her friends.

His down-home expressions, his Mario Lanza impersonation, they alarmed her, then charmed her. "Your vocabulary is richer than chocolate pudding," she mocked him.

"The cadence in your voice tickles me."

Louie turned to the side and faked embarrassment. "Hell, I don't talk no different from nobody else. We may be horses of a different color, but we're all eggs in the same basket."

Lorraine laughed. "You sound like my dad."

Now, Louie was gone, like the other ones. Gone, and with him the smell of fresh basil, the boxes of potato chips, the apple cookie jar. And she was alone. Like the Lorraine she knew best. The phone rang.

"What's wrong?", her mother asked. "I can tell by your voice there's something wrong."

"Louie left."

Silence. Then, "How long did he last? Since last winter? You and *Time* magazine ought to get together on your Man of the Year."

"I wasn't asking for sympathy, Mother."

"That's good. Because I don't have any. Not for you after two marriages and more affairs than I can count. You couldn't even get along with your father."

Lorraine thought about Dad. No word from him since he walked away. Maybe dead, maybe alive. She remembered the last day she saw him, standing in the kitchen of the duplex in St. Cloud. He was stirring spaghetti sauce, wearing a red silk Hawaiian shirt and Elvis Presley sideburns. She was a high school senior and had argued with him over a weekend curfew. Her mother leaned over the sink, washing dishes, keeping her distance.

"Well, Mother," her dad had said. "Are you going to support me on this one?" He tilted his head at a quizzical angle.

Her mother turned and dried her hands on her apron. "I think you two can work it out."

"I don't think we can," he said. "I'm tired of being the lonely little onion in this petunia patch." Next morning, he was gone.

"He'll be back," her mother said. "He's done this before."

But he didn't return. Lorraine replayed the conversation, regretted her insolence, felt distance between her and her mother. Over coffee one morning, her mother had said, "If you hadn't been such a bitch . . . "

Lorraine met Harold later that year. The fact that he was thirty-two and paid attention to her was flattering. He wanted children, he said. Lots of children. And she was the right age to fulfill his fantasy.

After the first night they spent together, she was convinced that she was pregnant. The symptoms her friends had discussed—dizziness, morning sickness, craving unusual foods—all of these presented themselves at confusing moments, in bewildering deportment. She confided in Harold, not her mother.

"We have to get married," Lorraine said. "As soon as I graduate." She had rehearsed this speech for days. "Mother will want a church wedding. The baby should be born around Christmas. If it's a boy, let's call him Harold Jr."

All of which played into Harold's plan. Later, the doctor told Lorraine that stress had caused her to miss her periods—her father's leaving, her mother's hostility, her graduation, Harold's arrival. The doctor offered his diagnosis before the wedding, and Lorraine accepted it as rational. But it was embarrassing to back out. Her friends would snicker, her mother would roll her eyes, Harold would be despondent. He had bought a Jenny Lind crib at a Used Furniture Store. Besides, she would likely be pregnant next month.

But she wasn't. When Harold heard the gynecologist say that Lorraine was infertile, and when she confessed the pregnancy ploy, he had the marriage annulled. Lorraine found a job as a switchboard operator at the telephone company and moved into a "No Men Allowed" boarding house.

She met Darrin a year later at a friend's wedding.

Bridesmaid Lorraine found the ceremony, the tempo, the gaudy extravagance intoxicating. Her speech and manner took on an affectation. A French braid was the *most* elegant; a bouquet was the *most* glorious; an organ prelude, the *most* breathtaking. It was in this giddy whirlwind that Lorraine met Darrin, the *most* handsome man on the groom's side, as voted by the women on the bride's side.

Lorraine danced with Darrin at the reception and found him, for her, comfortably uncomfortable. "Do you know this step?" she asked when the band played a waltz. When he didn't, she led. She felt new confidence, new determination, new power. "I'm warm," she said, lowering her dress off the rounds of her shoulders. "Let's get some fresh air."

Within months, they married, at Lorraine's suggestion. "He's so malleable," she told her friends. "One hundred and sixty pounds of Silly Putty. You want plain vanilla, he's plain vanilla. You want tutti-fruiti, he's tutti-fruiti. Nothing beyond tutti-fruiti though. Nothing bizarre. No imagination."

"Lorraine as dominatrix," her friends laughed. "Have you taught him to sit on the toilet instead of dripping pee on the floor?"

"I should. I'm tired of mopping up after him. I should. I will."

Lorraine returned from work to find a note on the kitchen table. "I can't seem to satisfy you," Lorraine read. "I tried to be charitable with you, to be flexible. But this old dog can't learn all those new tricks. I'll start the proceedings."

She met Luigi at an Italian cooking class, where they were assigned the salad course. Louie tore the lettuce with the fingers of a masseur, diced the tomatoes with staccato precision, sliced the onion paper thin, and tossed the ingredients with theatric abandon. Lorraine sipped Chianti and watched his fingers gently crumble the feta cheese and fondle the calamota olives.

"You like to cook, don't you?" she said at dinner.

"I allow myself one bad habit. Food."

And now, Louie was gone. The cast iron cookware, the German cutlery, the trays of herbs. The aroma of sauces when she walked in the door, the aria from *La Boheme*, the bear hug welcome. Gone. All gone.

Her mother joined her for coffee Saturday morning. "It's good to have the apartment to myself," Lorraine said. "No tripping over his stuff. No explaining if I want to go to bed at eight, and get up at three."

Her mother sipped coffee.

"I've had it with men," Lorraine continued. "The toilet seats left up. The Monday night football. The whiskers in the sink."

"You can't live with them, and you can't live without them," her mother said.

"I can live without them." Lorraine cradled her coffee cup and stared out the window. The phone rang.

"You're kidding," she said to the phone. "Two round trips to Vegas? Sure, I'll go." She listened. "I've never stayed at Caesar's Palace."

Her mother tapped her cup on the table and glared.

"Let me think about it," Lorraine said to the phone. "I'll call you tonight."

Poetry

by Jane Levin

change of pace

maple hula in full swing
jitterbug time
dignified limbs creak/betray
her years

rusty tissue papers crinkle
break away/drift
aloft freeze-dried gusts/touch
down in Key Largo
sway with fronds of palm
eavesdrop on bracts
            of brilliant bougainvillea
sink into pastry flour dunes

she slows to a winter waltz
marks time

Creative Nonfiction
by Russell W. Jacobson

Ants Toting Sugar Crystals, Beetles with Iridescent Wings

No implement is hooked behind or mounted on the scale-model Farmall in our living-room hutch. A John Deere diesel sits beside it, for which last year I bought a 214-T baler. A baler may be the heart of haymaking but mine took up too much space on my allotted shelf and I gave it away. What the heck, we never had a 214-T, only a rusty-red baler powered by its own motor because neither Farmall had live PTO. We never had a John Deere either, not while I lived at home. We had two Farmalls and a small Allis Chalmers C.

Still, there is something powerful about making hay—a task at once solitary and social. Perhaps I should add a hay mower, a hay wagon, a side-delivery rake. Windrowing a field is creating art, the rake's reel turning and tossing and braiding two mower swaths into one springy roll . . . such easy-pulling, half-throttle work.

My mind drifts from the perfume of alfalfa blooms, the sweet juice of cut stalks, the bouquet of sun-dried leaves—from the eye-stinging sweat of growing a stack. I am plowing now, raucous, hovering, ring-billed seagulls haunting my solitude. No rush to finish plowing the field; it can be finished tomorrow, the next day, or next week.

Last January I saw a 1/16th scale-model 4-bottom Oliver plow with hydraulic lift for $250. Neither of our Farmalls would have had power to pull it—the M pulled three 16-inch bottoms, the H only two. Neither had the two-way hydraulics needed for the Oliver plow. For us, tugging a rope attached to a lever on the plow's right wheel set in motion a cam that lifted the shares from the ground at the end of the field. After turning around, a second tug dropped the shares back into the ground. Too long a tug and the shares lifted and fell. Smell the turning loam, the slick clay.

There are so many possible implements from which to choose . . . a disk, a spring-tooth, or drag to smooth soil for seeding . . . the promises of seed drills and planters, powerful as a gambler's fever for luck . . . a mounted two-row corn cultivator; Lord knows the hours I spent driving up and down corn rows . . . a grain swather . . . a combine . . . dust, dust, dust to gold, dirt-caked faces cracked by smiles of fortune.

It wasn't only the Farmalls; with the Allis, I raked hay on the meadow where the ground was soft. And I used it to pull an old two-wheeled fencing trailer. It took two to fence across the river or into the lake—the river sheltered quietness scented by grass, weeds, and mud—the breezy-bright lake smelling of fish and sun-blanched rocks, silence broken by the tamping of posts, the creak of stretching wire, the pounding of staples, commands, and teasing soft enough to have been whispered in your ear—*Toss me the hammer. Don't let it drop into the river. Heard you got a letter this morning.*

Narrowing implement choices to one foments a rebellion of memories. And in fact, memories are what I seek, not resolution of them. I could say that even an unbridled toy tractor has pulled for me over the years, reminded me no job worth doing was too big or too hard—cautioned me to be careful of what loads I pulled.

In chronological fairness, I might represent my first tractor solo on the Allis. Dad hooked a rusty log chain to the draw bar, told me to drive the field road and don't come back till the chain shone. He had prepared me over the years by having me shine twisted-link chains of the seed drill's marking disks by pulling them behind a bicycle given us by Dad's brother, a spring-wheat big farmer from Kansas who spoke with a southern drawl. I think Dad was checking if I could drive forward and glance backward at the same time. Thinking of hooking a chain behind a tractor lugs me down. It reminds me of how as I once battled life, I had to hook onto misjudgments and failures and pull them out, how even now it's hard to let failure lie and move on instead of dragging it behind. Sometimes it's hard remembering what I pulled and what pulled me. In truth, some of my best tractor times were before hooking up and after unhooking.

Poetry

by Ronald Gower

Deja Vieux

In my recurring dream,
The draft has come for me
Again, and I am whisked
To basic training, despite
My wail at every stage
That I am now seventy,
And surely not a soldier
Any more.

And then I'm crawling
Through Fort Carson mud,
And carrying a combat pack
Filled for a giant, plus my old
M-1, and a metal helmet, and
The weight of fifty years
Since as a 'Cruit E-1 it all was
Just a game.

The heaviness this time
Is that I know what follows,
Know the rules, and when
The rules go wrong: the
Right way and the Army way.
And that machine gun is not
Firing at a cautious line
Above my head.

I die, of course, this time,
And I knew that too, that
Two is an unlucky number.
This time I will not have
Those fifty years forgetting
Or those times when I
Remember, when I hope
In my dream it is
Only a dream.

Poetry

by Sandra Edlund

Pheasant Under Grass

From the ruins of winter, a bright bird emerges from the forest.
Colorful and resplendent, he is a pauper prince against the gnarled
trees.
His head is emerald, his eye, ruby.
Under a weak sun, he struts and pecks at the dung-brown earth
Where the slate gray rocks hide a nascent spring.
Bird of prey, he skitters across my yard as if fleeing an imaginary foe.
But there is no hunter here.
Only my prying eyes admire his preening beauty.
Grass under pheasant,
Geese skidding across the ice.
Flat-footed ducks skim across open water.
Out of plodding winter,
Spring arrives on tiptoes.

Poetry

by Laura L. Hansen

At Night In Secret

At night, in secret,
The mushrooms rise,
Lift pale moon faces
To the dappled sky.

At night, in secret,
The mushrooms rise.
They lift their skirts,

They stretch and twirl,
And let their lace-edged
Slips unfurl.

All through the night,
They dance
On stile and stalk and stem.

Then toss their spores
Like bridal flowers
To waiting maiden earth.

By morning, when we rise,
The ghostly mushroom dance
Has passed.

Their caps are smudged
With black and crushed into
The mussed and tangled grass.

So rich the life,
So short the dance,
From first moon shine
To fruit to spore to ash.

Fiction
by Catherine Ritchie

But Not Forgotten

"Mommy!"

The cry cuts through me like a knife. Turning, I see the young boy, all blue eyes and soft, blond curls, face shimmering with fluid seeping from eyes and nose. He has just realized that all the knees around him belong to strangers.

I get down on his level, eye to eye. "What's your mommy's name?" I ask in a calm voice.

His swimming eyes focus briefly on me, and then resume scanning the area. "Mommy," he repeats, his voice fading in defeat.

I take his sticky hand gently. "What color shirt does your mommy have on?"

Slowly he returns his focus to me. A long moment passes, and I'm about to repeat my question, when he answers, "Blue."

Picking up the now dripping child, I carefully dab his face with a tissue from my pocket. "Let's go find Mommy."

With help from store security, it doesn't take long. "Mommy" is nearly as teary as her son. I leave them busily sobbing into each other and slip out into the late afternoon sun. Walking to my car, I can still feel the warmth and wetness of the child on my shirt.

"Mommy!" I seem to hear in the wind. I start my car and turn up the radio.

After supper, Bobo and I head out the back door, 'round the garden and into the woods. The dog wags his tail, happy to be outside. Today we head west, down toward the river that flows in the distance. Bobo is a whirl of energy, racing ahead, running in circles, sniffing everything, everywhere. We are both looking for a lost scent.

I pass my neighbor, Emma. She's out digging in the bean patch today. She waves and catches Bobo in a hug as he races up to her. I wave back and continue my walk.

"Susan?" Emma calls, "You okay?"

I nod, reluctantly stopping. "I want to look over by the river."

Emma's face clouds with concern. "It's been three years, Susan," she says carefully.

I don't want to meet her eyes, to see the pity there. "I know it's been three years. I need to look." I walk away without further conversation, Bobo bouncing alongside of me.

Three years. Three very long years. My daughter Missy would be seven this fall, going into second grade. She should be seven. Should be walking here with me, chatting away, laughing with the sunshine, chasing the butterflies. If it wasn't for that monster. How do you tell a three year old child there really can be monsters in the world?

He moved into our small town a year or so before Missy disappeared. Seemed a quiet type, withdrawn, kept to himself mostly. Worked at the lumber mill. He went missing the same day Missy did. I remember it was a beautiful spring day. Flowers were crowding the hills, bird song filling the air, the sky just calling for admirers to come out and enjoy the day.

Walking the path, I kick at a rock. I feel the rage boiling inside me, thinking about it. The panic, the frantic searching, police, dogs, neighbors forming human chains to canvas the town and the nearby lakes.

The man showed up again, a day or so later. When questioned, he denied any involvement. A search of his car showed traces of her DNA. Whether from tears or blood I don't know. I didn't want to know. I just wanted my child back.

I tried to see the man in jail, to talk to him. He hid in the shelter of bars and bricks, wouldn't meet my eyes in court. The evidence mounted, a past history uncovered. "Tell me where she is!" I pleaded.

A week before the trial, the bastard hung himself.

"Bastard," I repeat, under my breath. Bobo pauses, watching me for clues.

"Go find her, Boy." This has become my mantra. "Go find her."

The light is slowly fading as we round the bend of the river and start the long walk home. The spring floods were higher than normal this year, and the debris is still piled in spots. Part of the river's course has shifted southward.

I'm lost in thoughts when I hear a strange yip. Stopping, I see Bobo standing by a raised mound of earth near the river, covered with branches and flood debris. Bobo is focused totally on the dirt in front of him. I can see him trembling.

My legs feel like lead as I walk toward him. I can see the piled earth, the cracks where the flood had shifted the soil. Then I see the small, white bones.

Sinking to my knees, I gently reach toward the remnants of a small hand, the bones held together by gossamer threads of ligaments long dormant. For a moment the world dims, a fog swirls around me, and all I see are those delicate fingers, reaching out to me from far away.

Bobo bumps his head against my shoulder, hard. He forces his head under my arm and whines. Hugging him, I'm numb.

The wind lifts the hair off my back. "Mommy!" I hear again, faintly.

"It's okay, Missy," I murmur through my tears, "Mommy's come to take you home."

Poetry

by Sharon Harris

Alzheimer's

the fog slips in
on little cat feet—

no, no, that's been done before.
rather let's say that
cotton candy cobwebs
drift in from the lake
to clutch at the edges of my vision.

mist or fog,
smoke or smog,
or a combination
of them all—
what is it?

it slides around me
with choking closeness,
slinks into my mind
with its cloying moist silence.

it is so hard to think—
what is it?
insanity, depression,
indecision,
or plain and simple confusion?

Poetry

by Margaret Mary Gorman, SSND

Communion

Rejected by her mother in Texas,
given away by her grandmother in Mexico,
abandoned by her aunt in Minnesota,
divorced by husband,
spurned by daughters,

Juana roams the streets.
At noonday, near the library,
she finds a homeless man
eating bread. Respectfully
sharing his, she receives.

Poetry

by Barbara Jacksha

Witches' Dream

On rocky, barren shore, one
twisted tree where none belongs
    Spirit Tree to Ojibway
    Witch Tree to trappers, voyageurs.
No one knows her age;
sere and shrunken, roots
still splitting glacial stone.

November breathes ice—
witch limbs tremble.
I shiver with her, see
    hardened breasts
    bone-thrust hips
    reedy, rippled thighs.
Prickly fingers, white with
moss or frost point skyward;
she leans toward water—
one day she will dive.

That night, twig fingers slip,
her dream to mine. I see
    light shimmers
    like rare white bats
    skimming restless waves—
    the hag daughter's reflection.

Crone hands stir wind, rise to tap
the daughter's round, radiant face.
Witch needles rustle, whisper—
    Remember where you came from

Raven flies, arrow through light.
Silver-moon voice cackles back
    Always

Creative Nonfiction
by Bonnie West

Her Autobiography.

Or, at the Very Least, What She Thinks

Her autobiography, if she sticks only to religion, might well be about discovering the bliss of a new faith and then its certain disappointment, a process much like meeting one soul-mate after another, and though she's been married to the same man for more than thirty years, or perhaps because of it, she no longer believes in soul-mates, any more than she believes in Luther as the answer to Roman Catholic dogma, Jerry Falwell as the antidote to Protestant liberalism, or the Pope and his so-called infallibility. In fact, as far as the Pope is concerned, she finds herself on the other side of nearly every issue, especially those concerning women. Nor does she believe in the Hindu and Buddhist philosophies she tried on from time to time like cute shoes which were too snug but shoes she'd purchased anyway, hoping one day her feet might shrink.

But if she addresses spirituality, which she believes to be different from religion, although it can encompass religion when it must, a more interesting story might appear. She always felt, as she supposed most everyone must feel from time to time, confused and concerned about the answers to the questions being asked. The usual suspects: Is there a God? What happens when you die? What's it all about? (She can't help but think, *Alfie.*) But lately her questions have changed. Does it matter? And, who cares? But that is the end of the story and not the beginning.

Her grandmother, a Unity minister, christened her with rose petals. No, she doesn't remember being baptized, but she remembers well how strange rose petals seemed to everyone she told. So she made up a story of how her grandmother thought it kinder to press petals, than to dribble water, on a baby's brow.

Rose petals notwithstanding, she was raised Episcopalian and every night before sleep said the Twenty-third Psalm and the Lord's Prayer. Her father sat on the side of her bed and recited with her until it was known. She's forgotten the Psalm but each night the Lord's

Prayer rises without intent into her mind and she refuses to sleep until she has said every word, paying strict attention to each one and its meaning. How much she hates forgiving those who trespass against her, even slightly. How now she finds she no longer believes in Father or heaven or his kingdom coming. Some nights she repeats the prayer hoping for symbolism but is certain Jesus meant it literally. She no longer believes Jesus is God. "I can't believe unless I feel the wounds," she thinks. Poor doubting Thomas: once a loving disciple of Jesus and now a cliché. She always identified with Thomas.

In college, she turned Catholic for a priest. Such unremitting love, she skipped episodes of *Star Trek* for Tuesday night Instruction. She protested with the priest against the War in Viet Nam, and traveled hand in hand with him to Washington to march for Martin Luther King. Then she sadly played the mandolin at his wedding to a girl like her, 'tho sweeter. But that was long ago, far from this present point and her utter loss of faith.

She believes demise of faith is caused by chemicals, or better said, the lack thereof. A simple liquid, one time coursing through her veins, has now run dry. The change of life, the leach of estrogen from blood and bones, has also dried her soul. Artificial hormone creams for lusciousness, she *thinks* might conjure God again but she'll never know. She will not even try. Cancer risk is high. "Natural cures" like witches' warts and batwings mulled in wine have failed to bring her back in line. She's all dried up.

The loss of faith is curious, the loss of sex is crushing; she pines for sexy days gone by. Men no longer look at her, nor really, she at them. The steamy sexiness, the heat, the lusty longing, is simply, sadly, gone. She contemplates the loss of faith and sex and wonders then, what else is gone? Not appetite, that's hearty! Nor politics, her zest remains robust. She misses Bill the sexy president and bets a kiss from him would prime the pump, but the likelihood of meeting Bill? More likely that the Virgin will appear.

Oh, how, so long ago, she desired that. A trip to Majegore where the Virgin might appear. Oh, how she dreamed of Majegore, her beaded rosary, and alchemy; she clutched it to her breast. She believed the tales and asked herself, *Which would you rather have? A vision of the Virgin or a rosary of gold?* Then a nasty game played in her mind, *Which would you rather be: deaf or blind, armless or legless, anorexic or morbidly obese?* But the answer to the first was easy: *See the Virgin. See the Virgin.*

All that is past. She no longer thinks of rosaries or visions of the Virgin, nor does she want or miss them. Once, when asked if there were freedom in the loss of faith, she answered, "Yes, oh yes."

But now she must reevaluate these things and many more: the car crushing the bike but not the boy; the cheating lover; the blue-ribbon pie; the house haunting; the ruptured spleen; the dying child; fire in the basement; the murdering friend; dogs rescued from the river; an in-the-park home-run; the heart attack. Oh, all the near misses and close calls: the good, the bad, the in-between. Not God, not God. Just chance.

Poetry
by Annette Marie Hyder

Boundaries

He touches me
and I see tiny fire goblins
dancing around my wrist
a live action bracelet
howling with desire
where he laid his hand.
His eyes are twin Lucifers
burning darkly for me—
flaming hoops to jump through.
For what? I ask myself.
Because you can, he tells me
although I have not spoken
that question out loud.
To get to what is on the other side,
he adds and he holds out his hand
a flaming brand to light my way.
I think of the circus—
not the shiny pretty Cirque du Soleil
art nouveau kind of circus
rather the gritty kind, the dirty kind
with freaks and gimps and tragedies.
I turn on my heel, am not interested
in the kinds of tricks that he would have me do.
My steps are s – l – o – w
like in dreams and I know that every one I take
ignites, match-like, strange connections between me
and him—my very good friend's husband.

Creative Nonfiction
by Pat Spilseth

Ice House Romance

Though the sky was filled with billowing, white snow clouds, glaring rays of sunshine blanketed the pristine whiteness of the frozen lake. Gazing out the kitchen window, I squinted, shielding my eyes from the painful brilliance. A few ice houses huddled in tiny village formation just beyond my shore line. Fishermen anticipated the capture of Wally the Walleye. I imagined a lone fisherman slouching on his stool inside, drinking countless cups of coffee to stave off the icy chill, relishing his independent solitude.

What lures men to these ice caves of silent loneliness? I've always wondered, but never understood, why is there such spell-binding romance about the idea of sitting with a fishing pole in a cramped shack on the frozen ice? Why would anyone want to endure the freezing discomfort of slipping on icy paths, cracking a few bones, or spraining an ankle or two on the unforgiving ice floor, to get to their isolated cave? Early in the season, it's too dangerous for vehicles to cart bodies out to these ice villages, so fishermen have to dress in bulky overshoes, fleece-lined snow pants, down-filled parkas, insulated gloves, and wool hats to reach their havens. But fishermen dream of this treacherous ice pursuit all week long. On weekends, they forage for fish, enjoying the quiet isolation and kerosene warmth of their cramped ice cave.

Trust me, it's more comfortable and cheaper to buy a fish dinner at a restaurant or fish at the grocery store downtown. Who needs such miserable discomfort for a simple bite of walleye?

But the cave man syndrome continues, even in modern day society. Men, romanticized as strong, silent warriors, long to be respected providers and protectors of their womenfolk. Imagining themselves to be heroic hunters and trappers starring in adventure paperbacks, they feel a strong obligation to "bring home the bacon" to Mama and the kids. Forget the fact that many of these same "cavemen" on the frozen lakes also work a sixty or seventy hour week in addition to their weekend "fishing duties."

But ice house issues differ vastly from issues raised within the home with the family. Slipping off to the quiet solitude of his romanticized cave, a man doesn't have to concern himself with family problems of barking dogs, curfew-busting kids or answering such thought-provoking female questions such as "How much do you really love me?" and "What do you think about booking a trip to Paris or Tahiti?"

Today's man can retreat to the perfect haven from worldly problems. The fish house, with its cold comfort, provides the proverbial cave of yesteryear. The aura of being a hunter and provider lures many bespectacled accountants, plumbers, classroom teachers, ministers, and bankers to dark ice houses far out on the frozen lake. Alone time means no nagging, no duties, no reminders of what needs to be done.

Problem solved: I'll go fishing!

Poetry
by LuAnne White

Headache

Someone is pounding on my backbone,
pouncing upon my brainwaves.
Chasing my thoughts, once organized,
into mad, wispy whirls
rabbits across a field
looking over their tails
to see if someone follows their fright.

Poetry
by Julie C. Larson

My Anger

My anger eats thunder for breakfast
    and brushes its hair with lightning.
My anger wears hurricanes on its fingers
    and comets in its ears.
Its teeth are sheer granite cliffs
    and when it smiles, continents tremble.
It breathes hot ash, molten rock
    and sighs oceans into deserts.

My anger is beyond time, beyond space.
It grips history in its left hand,
    the future in its right,
    like two ticking bombs.
With one mighty laugh it claps its hands
    and sweeps the world clean.

Poetry
by Shirley Ensrud

The Lesser Evil

I am a puppet without strings
as they pass me from room to room,
from receptionist to nurse, doctor,
lab tech, EKG and X-ray technicians.
Weight—129, temperature 99.6,
Blood pressure—160 over something.
Dr. McCarty reviews my file,
"Do you feel—? Have you had—?"
prods, looks, listens.

They control my movements,
insist on changes of costume—
capes with front or back openings.
"Roll up your sleeve. Just a little prick.
Sorry." She fills three vials.
"Remove clothing above your waist."
A dozen cold, round stickies attach wires
to arms, legs, chest, sides.
Now I truly am a marionette.
"Just sit back and relax."

Russell had triple bypass last week,
Gordon six months ago.
Merle never survived his.

"Stand with your chest against the board.
Take a deep breath, inhale, hold, hold, hold, exhale.
Stand with your shoulder against the board.
Deep breath, ho-o-o-ld, exhale.
Wait in the chair while I see what we got."

Doctor says, "Everything looks fine.
Take these capsules for acid reflux disease.
Its symptoms do resemble heart attack.
I will retake your blood pressure.
129 over 58." She smiles.
"It is always better when you can relax."
She sends me home, a real person again.

Creative Nonfiction
by Niomi Rohn Phillips

Deer Season

It's Saturday, two weeks before "The Opener," and it is rush hour on my barely-a-road walking trail. Pickups carrying lumber go by; the drivers smile, wave. Men on ATVs roar through my autumn quiet, waving as they pass. They flag trees, marking trails, pound their deer stands together in my woods.

I have been trying to understand the *Deer Hunting* phenomenon all my adult life. What is the fervor all about? Maybe it's like spring for me. When I open the door one April morning at sunup, and the woodland winter silence is broken by birds flitting from tree to tree, calling their greetings, I am awash with joy. Or Christmas? When decorated trees appear in Fleet Farm and holiday music accompanies me even in the grocery store, I walk with a lighter step and smile at everyone I meet. Maybe deer hunters feel like that when blaze orange hats, jackets, and shirts appear in their favorite sporting goods stores along with the fresh chill of fall.

I didn't grow up with hunters, so I was ignorant of the rituals, the bonds, the culture involved. The first time I spent a weekend with my fiancé's family, and he asked his grandmother to repair his hunting coat, I was too naive to see the blaze orange flag.

A couple of years later, I was too astounded to protest when father-in-law Ted dragged a deer head out of the trunk of his car and hauled it into our house. "Monte's brother has always wanted this trophy head," he said, "but he's in Seattle, and you can't chance shipping something this valuable."

Lucky for his wife, I thought.

Monte revered that trophy. His dad shot that deer in 1954. Four men and a boy dragged it through the woods. The head was mounted by a famous taxidermist and hung prominently in the club room of the local Elks Club . . . until it found a home with us. Monte and his dad had the perfect place to hang it in our house, the obvious place, they said—right next to the fireplace in the dining room.

The rack *was* a topic of dinner conversation. Male dinner guests had endless discussions about the size of the animal and where it was shot, the impressive number of points, the Boone & Crockett caliber of the head. Their wives would light another cigarette and smile tolerantly. It was definitely a man thing.

I did resent having that head in my dining room. For fifteen years, a tall friend commented on it every time she walked in the house. "I can look that thing right in the eye."

The kids helped me tie a red bow around its neck at Christmas and hang bells from the twelve points. Father-in-law Ted wasn't amused.

When we built our cabin, I suggested we hang the trophy head there. Ted sputtered—indignant, appalled. Somebody would surely break in and steal it. That seemed most unlikely to me, but we didn't risk challenging him, so it stayed in the dining room.

After Ted died, we took the trophy head to our cabin. It fit perfectly between two lofty windows, so I didn't have to look at it, unless someone called attention to the cobwebs lacing the rack. And the rack was again a catalyst for conversation. New male acquaintances would look up, comment on the pine paneling, then rest their eyes on the deer head. That gave them entrée for the exchange of hunting stories.

One Friday night in winter '97, we saw truck tracks in the fresh snow as we turned off the highway onto our narrow, winding road. The lights were on in the cabin, so we knew something was amiss. The front door was closed, but the big footprint dead center made the means of entry obvious.

Inside was havoc. Drawers were emptied on the floor in bedrooms, games in heaps in the living room, food pushed off pantry shelves. Television, stereo equipment, binoculars, and tools were gone; even the beds were stripped bare of their goose down. And the deer head. It had never enhanced the decor as far as I was concerned, but Monte was understandably distraught with its loss. The sentimental value was inestimable.

Ted was right again, I thought, *and is "up there" saying I told you so.*

We kept in touch with the sheriff's office the next couple months, but the robbery wasn't solved. Then one Saturday in April, the sheriff called soon after we arrived.

"I can't believe it," Monte said when he got off the phone. "A UPS delivery man found a deer head in the ditch and turned it in. It looks like mine."

Only in Minnesota. The trophy rack is back on my wall. I live with it permanently now. And last year a son-in-law saw fit to have his trophy deer head mounted. Since it was too big for his own house, he hung it in my bunk room. Its head is canted, the glass eyes facing the top bunks. Granddaughters say it freaks them out. Grandsons think it is "cool." The fraternity of deer hunters lives on.

Poetry – Honorable Mention
by Ronald Gower

Myownhorn

When I was young I was forced to take
Piano lessons, which I hated until I
Didn't have to take them, after
Which I loved to play piano.

And I played and played and played
Until one day when I was older I
Heard George Shearing do the
Same thing, only not,
And I knew I
Was just
Playing.

I loved the sound of jazz trombone,
So I learned how to breathe again
And how to fill that plumbing
Full of air, and make it slip
And slide, and then at the
Prom Ballroom, I
Heard Tommy
Dorsey.

Next day I picked up an old guitar,
And for the next three years I
Worked to harden finger tips,
To strum and stroke and
Make it sing, and this
Is it, I thought, until
An old man named
Segovia walked
Across the frets
Like an angel
From hell
And

That was that.
Now I think I
Will just make
Something else
And patent it
And no one else
Will be allowed
But me to blow.

Poetry

by Joanne Morén

Fall Serenade

Composed by a master,
directed by the wind,
autumn's chorale begins:
Sturdy, sunset hued
maple and oak
sing melody
and harmony.
Florescent aspen, yellow birch,
trill a soprano descant.
Pianissimo swells smoothly
to fortissimo,
slowly diminishes
into silence.
After a short intermission,
yellow tamarack and stately pine
commence winter's encore.

Poetry
by Scott Stewart

cool jazz

cool jazz
razzamatazz
drum that drum
hit that horn
soothe that sax
snap it fast

red light
jewel sitter
break a heart
blame her
quit her

cigarette haze
lazy gaze
sound a dream as
the instruments play

cool jazz cats
slap it back

cellophane pain
mainline vein
spoon and flame
in a cool jazz game

jade skin lure
half night tour
ten-spot talk
left turn door
slack hack war
slap ass whore

cool jazz has
cool jazz has

crackerjack razz

face it
case it
lace it
taste it

cool jazz has
cool jazz has

forbidden heat

cancer sweet
turn a trick
curse the treat
concrete needle
bleeds the street

cool jazz fade
tattered shade
midnight's paid
as it's laid

soiled sheet tent
ten-spot spent
cat trap capped
one room rent

cool jazz fell
cool jazz fell

hemp held cell
lies to tell
touch to sell
cool jazz hell

cat kick
cold pick
quick lick
MUSIC

cool jazz led
stained bride wed
lost life dead
cool jazz led
cool jazz led

Fiction
by Brenda Hill Seaman
My Hapless Husband

Two years after my husband retired, I staggered out of bed, eyed him sitting at the kitchen table, and decided to kill him.

"Good morning," he almost sang, looking up from his paperback with his usual smile.

Sloshing coffee into my cup, I didn't answer, didn't even glance at his smiling face. I was afraid I'd throw the hot coffee at him.

How could anyone be so bright and cheerful at six in the morning?

And why didn't he sleep late at least one time? Any sane person who didn't have to get up would be snuggled in a warm bed with the covers pulled up to their chin. If I didn't have to meet a printing deadline for our town's newspaper, I'd certainly be in bed.

When we were married twenty-four years ago, I'd adored him. As a systems analyst for large companies in the Midwest, Nick traveled several days each month, and when he returned home, we played like newlyweds. I'd never been so happy.

"Want some breakfast?" he asked, rummaging in the fridge for eggs and bread to toast. "I'll scramble an extra egg if you want," he added. "I know you're going to have a long day."

Not ready to talk and certainly not able to stomach food so early, I shook my head and managed a grunt.

"You should think about getting to bed a little earlier," he said, breaking eggs into a bowl and whipping them with a fork. "Those late night writing sessions take their toll."

I couldn't take it any longer, so, sitting at the table with my coffee, I planned his demise.

How could I do him in? I eyed his sturdy physique as he moved around the kitchen, popping bread into the toaster and dropping a pat of butter in the skillet. At almost six and a half feet, he could trace his lineage nearly to the Vikings. Plopping on his favorite western hat and donning his leather vest and gloves, he loved to roam the woods surrounding our northern Minnesota property, building fences to keep the deer out of the garden and chopping wood for our fireplace. Even at fifty-eight, he could outwork anyone, including my younger Southern cousins.

So what could I do? I wasn't handy with guns, and with all the forensic technology, I wouldn't dare try poison. Perhaps I could climb a tree and jump him as he strolled below me. But then what? I didn't like all the blood and gore from knives, so I couldn't stab him. When we were first married, we'd made a deal—I loved fresh fish, but when Nick caught a mess of crappies or perch from the lake, he'd clean them and I'd gladly cook them any way he wished. The same deal applied when he went hunting for game. Raised in Atlanta, I believed meat should come in nice little packages prettily wrapped in cellophane. Now I was considered one of the best cooks in the county.

"You have that look in your eye," Nick said, sitting down with his full plate. His hazel eyes were full of laughter. "What foul deeds are you planning now? Thinking of dumping the printing press into the lake?"

I wanted to slug him. Years ago, not long after we'd settled into the house on the outskirts of Nick's small hometown, we decided that I wouldn't work full time. That was fine with me—I wanted the freedom to be home when he had some time off. To help the days pass while he was away, I'd tried gardening, but raised in an urban condominium, I pulled the vegetables as well as the weeds. Next was sewing crafts and several of my new friends tried to help me, but I hopelessly tangled every strand of thread I touched. Thinking it would help, Nick even bought a new sewing machine, but I stitched his fly to his back pocket. After several more failed attempts, I waited until two in the morning, then, guided by the full moon, loaded the machine in the back of the Blazer and dumped it into the lake.

When I realized that our town, population 735, didn't

have its own newspaper, relying instead on the one from the county seat almost thirty miles away, I started one. At first, there wasn't much to report, but, determined to find something, I started interviewing local residents about their lives. I was surprised to learn that we had a retired school music director as a neighbor, so after I badgered him for a couple of years, he finally gave in and held auditions for a local band. Now, thanks to the local carpenters, we have a bandstand by the lake, and once a week in the summer, our town, as well as our neighbors, is treated to some good, old-fashioned concerts. The irregular lot of musicians, ranging from seniors to middle school children, may not be ready for the New York Philharmonic Symphony, but when they strike up 'The Stars and Stripes Forever' in honor of our armed forces, they bring everyone to their feet in pride.

After two more cups of coffee, I felt I could face my makeshift newsroom in the garage. Just as I stood, Nick, who had finished his breakfast and was back to reading his paperback, grabbed my arm and pulled me onto his lap. Just to hang on, of course, I slipped my arms around his neck. He gave me a nice kiss, but I was in no mood to dally. Not before dawn even cracked and I had several pages of print to turn into a newspaper.

"I don't have time to play this morning."

"I happen to know you coerced my sister and several neighbors into helping," he said. "The threat of no more home-baked peach pies is mighty powerful around here. Besides, it's our anniversary and I have something to show you."

Thank God it was summer, because he pulled me out the back door and down the graveled lane toward the lake.

"Oh, for heaven's sake." I anxiously peered through the dark woods for black bear. Would they be out this early? Probably not. Any sane living thing would still be sleeping. "Where are we going?" I asked, picking my way over the gravel. I eyed my husband, forging on ahead. The inconsideration of that man was beyond belief. Maybe I could get by with poison after all. Perhaps some vile potion smeared on his toothbrush. I'd have to do some research.

As we neared the lake, I could smell the water, a slight fishy smell mixed with the scent of moist earth and rotting vegetation. Frogs bellowed in the pinkening dawn.

When moving to the area, I wasn't sure I'd like living so close to nature. A lake instead of a shopping mall? And where were the fast-food restaurants? But, I grew to love the water, adored spending a lazy afternoon in our motorboat, drifting along with my line cast for fish. I'd even learned to bait my own hook. I'd had to, because my boorish husband told me very early that if I wanted to fish, I had to learn to do everything by myself. Grudgingly, I did so, and now I could hold my own with the best fisherman.

The only problem was with my porcelain skin. Even underneath a wide-brimmed hat and long sleeves, my skin burned and peeled. While I loved our fourteen-foot motorboat, I drooled over the big pontoons, the flat-bottom boats that floated on the water like royal yachts. Each time one drifted regally by, I lusted after the canopy-shaded deck. Some of the floating palaces even included iceboxes and gas grills. Oh, what an extravagance, but one I'd happily indulge. If my husband had any regard for my skin, he'd make sure we had one. He was just worried that I'd go more often and catch more fish. Then he, the big game hunter, would wither in shame.

"Just a few more feet," Nick said, picking up the pace. I almost stumbled trying to keep up with him. A knife. That's what I'd use. I'd watched him dress fresh deer and the first thing he did was hang it from a tree. That's what I could do. I'd set a trap and laugh as he swung upside down.

We rounded the bend and arrived at the boat launch, the single lamppost burning through the morning fog. But my eyes were drawn to a beautiful twenty-five-foot pontoon, a big, silky red bow tied to one of the canopy's supporting beams, floating on the water next to our motorboat. Strung across the deck was a sign that said, "Happy Anniversary!"

Before climbing aboard, I threw my arms around my grinning husband and gave him a big kiss.

My husband wasn't so hapless after all. He would live another day.